D0282845

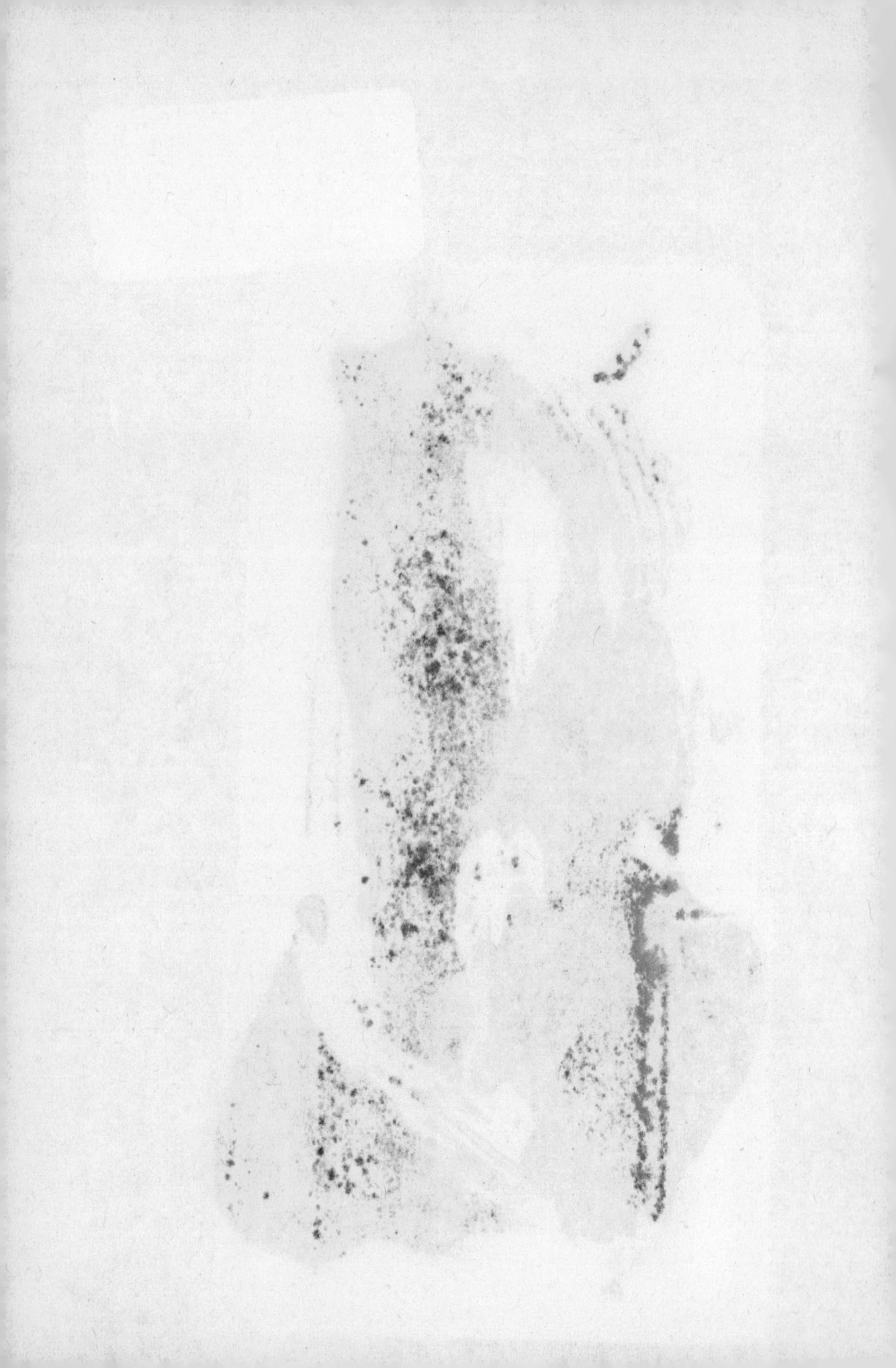

TWENTIETH CENTURY VIEWS

The aim of this series is to present the best in contemporary critical opinion on major authors, providing a twentieth century perspective on their changing status in an era of profound revaluation.

MODERN BRITISH DRAMATISTS

MODERN BRITISH DRAMATISTS

A COLLECTION OF CRITICAL ESSAYS

Edited by

John Russell Brown

Prentice-Hall, Inc.  *Englewood Cliffs, N.J.*

Acknowledgements

Quotations from John Arden's *Waters of Babylon, Live Like Pigs,* and *The Happy Haven* are printed by permission of the author and Penguin Books Ltd.; from his *Sergeant Musgrave's Dance* and *Armstrong's Last Goodnight* by permission of the author and Margaret Ramsay Ltd.; from John Osborne's *Look Back in Anger* by permission of the author, Faber & Faber, Ltd., and S. G. Phillips, Inc. (Copyright © 1957 by S. G. Phillips, Inc.); and from Harold Pinter's *The Collection* and *The Homecoming* by permission of the author, Associated Book Publishers, Ltd., and Grove Press, Inc. (Copyright © 1962, 1967 by Grove Press, Inc.)

 Library of Congress Catalog Card Number 68-14462. Printed in the United States of America.

Current printing (last number):
10 9 8 7 6 5 4 3 2 1

Preface

The view of the new British theater that this book gives, from numerous vantage points, is centered on those works of John Osborne, Harold Pinter, John Arden, and Arnold Wesker that were written in the nineteen-fifties and the first half of the sixties. In these plays can be seen both the breakthrough and the establishment of new modes of playwriting.

The four dramatists chosen for special consideration cannot represent all that is new in British theater and so the introduction and several of the following essays take a more general view. Because of their influence in style and experimentation, Samuel Beckett and John Whiting are given somewhat greater attention than others, although Beckett works in Paris (and mostly in French) and Whiting is not strictly "new" despite his association with the later generation.

The studies that comprise the book represent the best of the sustained critical comment that has appeared in books and journals. Newspaper reviews, although often perspicacious and exciting, have not been included, the object being to give a considered view, relating one play to others and one author to others, rather than the immediate impact of each new work. Nevertheless I should be greatly disappointed if something of the shock of new recognition and even of the bafflement of a critic confronted by original and imaginative work was not communicated through this book. Indeed it is my belief that the attempt to relate new works to each other and to our understanding of man, society, and history is the only effective way of preserving and harnessing the flash of revelation.

J. R. B.

Contents

MODERN BRITISH DRAMATISTS

Introduction

by John Russell Brown

We have in Britain, yet again, a new theater. Wherever a play is performed in a new production there is, of course, renewal, but at certain times everything becomes more obviously new: it was so in Shakespeare's age, during the Restoration, at the end of the eighteenth century, and at the end of the nineteenth: and so, again, today.

There is a new style of acting: less polished, perhaps less virtuoso; but stronger, more direct and individualistic, more related to behavior outside the theater. And new acting schools: the dominance of the Royal Academy of Dramatic Art, of the London Academy of Music and Dramatic Art, and of the Central School is being challenged by the new Theatre Centre School, by the East 15 School, and by the studio work of the Royal Shakespeare Company. And new stage design: architects (John Bury and Sean Kenny) and designers with a strong sense of texture (Jocelyn Herbert or, more recently, Christopher Morley) have ousted the painterly designers: there is a new sense of space, a new, efficient simplicity, and a new poetic solidity. And, above all, there are new plays and new dramatists.

Everyone seems to be writing plays: university students work in the theater and start writing plays instead of the poems or short stories which used to be the usual forms for expressing artistic originality; teachers, journalists, and housewives turn dramatists. (Olwen Wymark, a housewife with four children, had her first play performed in 1966 at the Citizens' Theatre, Glasgow; and the following year a collection of her first three plays was performed and and published.) The more progressive companies in London are sent hundreds of typescripts every year, and they have to employ a special staff to cope with the reading and correspondence involved. Even small repertory companies usually stage one, two, or three new plays not seen before in London or anywhere else, in each season's program.

The new plays have been given all sorts of labels: "kitchen-sink drama" was one of the first; neo-realist; drama of non-communication; absurd drama; comedy of menace; dark comedy; drama of cruelty. But no cap has fitted for more than a year or two; none has been big enough for more than one or two heads; and often the caps seem more suitable for the journalists who invent them than for the dramatists on whom they are thrust. Perhaps the first thing to say about the new dramatists is that they keep the critics on the run.

To understand the new movement, we must look beyond individual plays. If a dozen of the best were chosen, they would have remarkably little in common; each would need its own critical terms. The common ground is in determined experiment and innovation rather than any single theatrical means: in the kind of men the new dramatists are, their motives for writing plays, their choice of subject matter, rather than in any concentrated program or common achievement. First of all, they are young. They start writing for the theater early, after a few plays for radio or television, or a few abortive poems or novels; some of them dive straight in at the deep-end with a three-act play. Pinter, Wesker, Osborne, Arden—or more lately Edward Bond, David Cregan, Charles Wood, Joe Orton—had their first London production in their twenties—usually by twenty-four or twenty-five: by the mid 'sixties none of them is yet out of his thirties. Established writers in other genres (like the novelists Graham Greene or Angus Wilson), or established dramatists (like J. B. Priestley or Christopher Fry) have written for the theater in the last ten years or so, but none has risen with the new tide. In fact, they usually say, quite openly, that they do not want to.

Secondly, they like to be sensational; to surprise and shock; to be fantastic, unlikely, outrageous. (And this has often brought them into collision with the Lord Chamberlain, whose task it is to censor new plays for indecency and profanity.) In N. F. Simpson's *Resounding Tinkle* a character is announced as Uncle Ted: and when he enters he is a tall, dark, attractive woman, stylishly and carefully dressed, who at once accepts a considerate invitation to have a short read of a book or two. In Pinter's *The Room* a woman suddenly goes blind while speaking to a Negro. In Wesker's *Four Seasons,* a play with only two characters, the man spends about ten minutes carefully and often silently making an apple strudel on stage; and the woman, in a scene carefully hedged by the Lord Chamberlain's instructions, bares her breasts in order to be embraced. In Anne Jellicoe's *The Knack,* two characters play with great abandon on a bedstead as if it were a concert grand. In Edward Bond's *Saved* a baby is stoned to death in its perambulator on the open stage. Homosexuality, nymphomania, prostitution and abortion, violent or casual deaths, disfigurement, and callow humor are all part of the new drama.

Thirdly, the new writers frequently choose popular, up-to-date, topical, vulgar, very obvious subjects—as their contemporaries say, theirs is a "pop" art. Many of them write or adapt plays for television when they must consider an audience of millions; and they also work on film scripts. Of course in the theatre they do not have to please millions in this way—there an audience of thousands is sufficient; but their subjects are directly relevant to the same millions, are recognizably "pop." Pinter's *Collection* is partly about a collection of fashion-clothes and of a collection—very much in vogue in women's glossy magazines—of antiques. Wesker's *Chips with Everything* is about the service of conscripts in the Royal Air Force; his *Their Very Own and Golden City* is concerned with new housing projects and the ways of bureaucracy. John Arden's *Live Like Pigs* is about slum clearance, his *Workhouse Donkey* about local government. Ann Jellicoe writes about street gangs and girls alone in London looking for the Y.W.C.A. Pinter borrows subjects from suspense films (he is an admirer of Hitchcock), from television serials, and from the music hall, radio, and TV comedians. Charles Wood and Henry Livings take the army, factory workers, or a popular actress as subject matter, and use song, dance, soap-box oratory, pantomime, and the techniques of television commercials.

Perhaps more significant than all this, the new dramatists are firmly based in the theater. Pinter and Osborne were both actors before they turned dramatists—Pinter having a particularly varied career in McMasters' travelling repertory company. (Pinter still acts or directs when he can find time, but he has given up directing his own plays because his casts treated him with too much deference and because his productions became overcomplicated from his knowing too many things that could be done with his scripts.) Of the still younger generation, Charles Wood, Edward Dyer, Henry Livings, and Joe Orton have been actors. John Arden was trained as an architect but, marrying an actress, became immersed in theatre work, occasionally acting or directing with semiprofessional groups or schools. Ann Jellicoe taught at an acting school and has codirected her own plays.

Having written successful plays these authors do not go off and write novels or poetry; nor much criticism or journalism. They do work for television, radio, or films, but return again and again to the theater itself. Arnold Wesker became a dramatist after numerous jobs—much of the time he was a pastry-cook—but since writing plays he has become the administrative head, and chief fund-raiser and propagandist, for Centre 42, a play-producing Trust backed by the Trade Unions. He now understands the business of running a theater from the inside.

In the 1960s there has been an extension of the dramatists' link with theaters; perhaps one should say a "reaction" to it. For now several dramatic entertainments have been made anonymously, developed by a company during improvisations and rehearsals, sometimes with a dramatist, sometimes without one. Most successful, in the eyes of the critics, has been the Royal Shakespeare Company's *US,* a program on the Vietnam War. With Denis Cannan as script-writer, Peter Brook as director, and the actors as creative contributors, the play evolved from documents, improvisations, observations, and rehearsals: it was a group response in theatrical terms. This would have been unimaginable ten years ago in England, when the author was regarded as a gentleman who delivered finished products to an attentive producer. The new dramatists are not only closer to the theater; the theater has claimed them, and may even threaten to overwhelm the weaker ones.

How important are the new British dramatists? Will their work last? The question is important and difficult. The qualities that they share as writers do not reassure us: instead of being viewed as young, shocking, "pop," and theatrical, they might just as easily be characterized as immature, sensational, ephemeral, and stagey. They lay themselves wide open to destructive criticism, and they have taken a good deal of punishment from authoritative and experienced critics.

But an appeal to history can help, for the Elizabethan theater in which Shakespeare worked also had a throng of dramatists who were young, shocking, "pop," and very closely connected with the theater.

Marlowe, Jonson, Greene, Marston, Dekker, Heywood, Shakespeare, and Beaumont and Fletcher all started writing for the theater in their twenties. Marlowe and Greene died young, at twenty-nine and thirty-four respectively. All Jonson's best work for the theater was written by his mid-thirties; he continued as a writer, influential critic, and purveyor of court masques for many years, but none of his later plays has remained in our repertoires like his earlier *Everyman* plays, his *Alchemist, Volpone,* and *Bartholomew Fair*. Shakespeare had begun writing plays by the time he was twenty-six—some scholars believe he started three or four years earlier than this: *Hamlet* was written in his mid-thirties. He was exceptional among his generation in carrying on, writing successful plays until his forty-seventh year.

And the Elizabethans were sensational. To some extent their age, used to public executions of great cruelty and with memories of the fires in Smithfield during the religious persecution of the reign of bloody Mary, was less shockable or less tender than our own; and it may have accepted pain and suffering more readily. But by their own standards, their plays were shocking: the title-pages of printed editions proclaim "extreme cruelty," "lamentable tragedy," "odious death," "pitiful murder," "wicked abominations," "unsatiable desire of filthy lust," and the like. And cruelty was often handled in a manner that dwelt precisely on pain and outrage: the deliberation with which first one eye of Gloucester is gouged out on the stage in full view of the audience, and then the other, and the unfeeling physical language accompanying this action—"out vile jelly"—are hard to parallel in any play of western civilization. And for more headlong cruelty, consider the gloating rape and mutilation of

Lavinia, the hero chopping off his own hand on stage, and then his cutting of Chiron and Demetrius' throats on stage while Lavinia catches the blood in a bowl held between the stumps of her arms; and then, remember, as Titus himself puts it, "how daintily he plays the cook" in serving up to a mother her two sons baked in a pie—almost certainly a conscious outstripping of the Thyestian banquet of Seneca's play: all this in Shakespeare's early tragedy of *Titus Andronicus.*

And more than this, plays dealt with shocking moral subjects: sodomy in Marlowe's *Edward II;* blasphemy—for the Elizabethans a terrible matter—in a whole line of Tamburlaine heroes; incest in plays by Fletcher, Webster, and Ford; necrophilia in various degrees, and many strange conjunctions in love and sex, including a special exploitation of dances of men dressed as lewd animals. From this kind of sensationalism many of the most enduring plays of that time spring—for example, the penetrating exposure of the fantastic, sexual, and aggressive depths of the conscious and unconscious minds of Hamlet or King Lear.

The Elizabethan dramatists were "pop" too. They were forbidden by censor from representing reigning English princes on the stage, but they freely adapted history to topical ends. Queen Elizabeth herself was of the opinion that Richard II in a contemporary play of that name was intended by the author and actors to represent her own person. Enemy kings were more openly presented, as Philip of Spain in Lyly's *King Midas* or the entire Spanish Court in Middleton's *A Game at Chess* during James I's reign; this play had a record run of nine performances before it was censored, and then it enjoyed further life as a book. *Arden of Feversham* and *The Yorkshire Tragedy* were plays written to satisfy public interest in real-life domestic atrocities—"News of the [current, everyday] World." Into *Macbeth* Shakespeare wrote a topical concern with witchcraft and titbits from the accounts of the trial of Father Garnet following the Gunpowder Plot of the previous year; for *King Lear* he used a sensational pamphlet that displayed the "egregious popish impostures" of real-life confidence tricksters. In *The Tempest* Shakespeare reflected in detail a current interest in the colonization of Virginia, and he seems to have had access to an important newsletter before it had been published in any other form.

Like the new British dramatists, the Elizabethans worked in closest contact with the theatre companies. Two of the very greatest were actors before becoming writers: Ben Jonson and Shakespeare. Heywood was an active shareholder in one actors' company throughout his career. John Lyly ran his own boy-players. Several inductions, or prologues, show the actors to have been familiar with their author's ways, and he with theirs. Until after 1600, dramatists were directly and wholly dependent on the actors' companies, having no further financial interest in their work after they had pleased those who were to perform it.

Perhaps the weightiest argument that has been advanced against the claims of the new British dramatists for our attention is that they seem to write from no deeply-considered moral, social, or political purpose. Certainly it would be hard to gather from their works any considerable body of responsible opinion on these, or any other, matters. Their characters seldom debate the nature of existence or of society, like the protagonists of M. Sartre, or Mr. J. B. Priestley, or the late T. S. Eliot. There are two apparent exceptions to this, John Arden and Arnold Wesker. Arden's characters do talk about the nature of war and liberty, the conflict of public and private good; but these discussions are not the climactic scenes of the plays. Moreover, they explore and present a moral situation from several viewpoints, rather than speak for their author's opinions. The climax of an Arden play is usually a confrontation, or dance, or celebration, or, as in *The Workhouse Donkey,* a defeat of one party in the knowledge that neither side has made a permanent impression on the other, or on itself. Wesker does provide characters who speak for him—indeed all his plays have been accepted as autobiographical accounts of his own attempt to find a responsible role for the artist in society; but when this is acknowledged it is usually acknowledged sadly, for the theatrical life of his plays is not in the long discussions but rather in what he himself has called "demonstrations." Wesker has taken particular delight in a scene without a single word in *Chips with Everything* where he has "demonstrated," without argument and almost without subsequent comment, the effect of imposing one man's will on that of his fellows.

There has been no manifesto from the new dramatists, no proclaimed and commonly agreed program. Pinter has said that he does not find much to interest him in politics. Arden has made various unequivocal pronouncements, but on subjects like whether to use verse or prose, or on the role of a provincial repertory company. Osborne made his declarations as "an angry young man," in the '50s, and his first plays have some political comment; but his letters to the press are now most impassioned when he inveighs against the ignorance and blindness of dramatic critics. Generally the new dramatists distrust statements and definitions—I suspect that this is because they are thoroughly theatrical writers who know that words change meaning according to how they are said, by whom, to whom, in what place, whether sitting or standing or running, spoken slowly or quickly. These dramatists are not without serious purpose; indeed it is so serious that they will not attempt to express it in any other medium than the complicated and sensitive one of the theater.

In their exploitation of theatrical possibilities they show every sign of intellectual and responsible involvement. As I have said before, they are always eluding critical labels; and they are remarkably diverse in their achievements. This, I think, is the proper kind of responsibility for a dramatist. (Even Shakespeare has been reprehended for writing as if without any "serious moral purpose.") And their work is closely attentive to the society in which they live. The plays reflect "pop culture," but are not part of it. (The polemical Wesker has eloquently attacked the provision of brash, easy, repetitive entertainments and advertisements that can be assimilated easily by millions, in a lecture "On Building the House" published in *Encounter*.) They all *use* pop elements in their plays, but criticize and evaluate them by dramatic presentation and context rather than by argument. They acknowledge the cruelty and dangers around them by showing and controlling cruelty and danger in their plays. Many of them have remarkably alert ears for contemporary speech, so that their characters, even in farcical or absurd situations, are received by their audiences as pictures of themselves. (Pinter is the master of this accuracy, to such effect that it is now an everyday expression to say of a conversation "That was Pinter dialogue.")

By opening any volume of the Penguin *New English Dramatists* one can see that in themes, characters, settings, real-life behavior, dialogue, the new dramatists are obviously responding to the society in which they live. But to judge the responsibility of that response, the progress of individual dramatists must be observed in some detail, especially in the discovery of new dramatic form. Osborne, Pinter, and Wesker provide three very different examples.

Osborne's first plays were structurally conventional: *Look Back in Anger* and *Epitaph for George Dillon* are three-act plays set within realistic walls like most of their immediate predecessors. Exposition, development, and conclusion, clear character presentation and progressive building of conflict and tension are all duly there. What was new was the kind of life these plays mirrored in detail: Osborne's own world—young, uneasily married and loving—and its thwarted idealistic pretensions. All the conventional discretion, polish, and good manners of the English drama had gone; and there was no condescension—indeed there was a great show of sympathy—towards what his predecessors would have called "low" characters. Also, the central character in each was a misplaced artist, reduced to anger, double-talk and, temporarily, compliance. From this center, Osborne's later plays were to develop: the best of them are largely monologues, while the others use plot and situation to present an occasion for understanding and revaluation.

In *Luther,* the hero driven by his moral, sexual, and physical tensions brings terror and pain to himself and others; and this is viewed over against the misery and defiance of the Peasants' Revolt. For Osborne this was a Brechtian experiment in historical drama, but his was a play of display rather than a parable or exercise in dialectics. The frankly apologetic presentation of Maitland, the central character of *Inadmissible Evidence,* shows the same emphasis on the hero as in *Luther* and the earlier plays; but now the other characters and the setting itself have become more mobile and less conventially secure in presentation. Maitland's world is shown as *he* experiences it in his mind: one actress plays three parts—without disguise other than dress and manner of speaking—to show that Maitland is struggling with the same adversary all the time, that his dilemma is always in part his own, not that brought to him from the "real" world outside. So, too, his clerk becomes his client and his assistant his accuser; his daughter is held still and tantalizing before him, and what he sees in her can seduce his thoughts. Tempo and sequence of time are both fiercely irregular. Osborne has broken convention to center attention on his hero. But the continued interest in monologue is not all; to think that is to miss the most significant development. Osborne is no longer angry and defiant; he is asking for compassion and understanding and, more surprisingly to judge from his early work, has found a way of recreating in physically realizable language, the inner, half-conscious pressures within his hero. The nightmare of a defeated idealist is not easily admissible in the theatre; even more rarely is it presented in palpable and challenging form, rather than in soliloquy. (This is the technique of *Lear* over against that of *Hamlet,* or a means of fusing the comic and serious plots of *The Changeling* or *'Tis Pity She's a Whore.*)

In other plays—*A Patriot For Me, Plays For England,* and *A Bond Honoured*—Osborne creates groups around his central characters that display their situation in society and, with the last play (developed from one by Lope de Vega), in the tradition of Christian thought and feeling. From his first play onwards Osborne has been moving with difficulty and energy towards a wider and truer relationship with the world around him. The plays have been fantastic and accurately realistic; large and small; historical and contemporary; monologue and babel. This variety is bred of responsibility and growing knowledge, not of ease or mere success.

Harold Pinter is the most obviously consistent of new British dramatists: his settings remain relatively simple and taken from the world he lives in; his plays progress, with little plot development, but by a progressive revelation of inner tensions and appetites, towards a moment of clarification when (as he has described it) something is said that cannot be unsaid. His ear for the nonverbal qualities of speech and his eye for gesture or stage-business that is both usual *and* gripping, seemingly casual and yet revelatory, have given a similarity to the dramatic texture of all his plays. His interest in everyday ritual has also continued, from a birthday party to a homecoming, through seeking living-space, taking possession, or taking "care" of a room, to taking breakfast or lunch, taking orders, fulfilling routines, visiting, collecting, and so on. The development of Pinter lies in his manipulation of dramatic focus.

The Room and *The Birthday Party* at the beginning of his career present seven or eight people, each carefully introduced; but the plots of these plays center interest on single characters, Stanley and Rose. After this, Pinter severely reduced the number of characters, to two in *The Dumb Waiter* and three in *The Caretaker;* but now the plot balances the audience's interest between them. The dramatic action (borrowing techniques from television, film, and music) allows each in turn to hold the audience's attention alone: at the end of each play two characters face each other, both equally understood by the audience.

Shortly after these plays Pinter rewrote an autobiographical and unsatisfactory novel, first for radio and then for the stage. Here again, a single character is obviously dominant among a small group, but undisguised soliloquy is now used to reveal the fantasy of this man's mind; it is inhabited by dwarfs, and the play takes its name from these rather than from a character, setting, or event, as is usual for Pinter. By returning to a hero-centered drama he has complicated and enlarged the hero's presentation beyond that possible in the narrative structure of the earliest plays.

Then, for *The Lover,* Pinter restricted himself once more to two characters, but now one of them is both husband and lover; by insisting on one man fulfilling two contrary functions Pinter has found a way to give direct expression to irrationality and fantasy, and is here more obviously sensual and sexual.

This was an important technical advance, but Pinter went still further in *The Collection* and *The Homecoming*. He returns, here, to larger casts, first four and then six (or eight counting the two who are already dead but very influential in the action and alive in the minds of the characters). But now the dramatic focus is on all the characters. At the end of *The Collection* four people are still and silent on the stage, each equally significant to plot, theme, and character-presentation. Just before the end of *The Homecoming,* the most sensitive character—the one who most easily could become the center of attention—leaves the stage; and at the close of this play the five remaining characters are silent, all equally significant to plot, theme, and character presentation. Pinter's involvement with the world around him has led him to a more open acceptance of the fantasy and sexuality of inner life and to a wider and more interrelated view of character.

Arnold Wesker's first two plays, *Chicken Soup with Barley* and *The Kitchen,* broke all the rules. They are written like films. The setting for *The Kitchen* involves several large gas ovens, a butcher's table, storage units, sinks, swing-doors—the whole apparatus of a large kitchen serving a busy restaurant. It is inhabited by thirty people: cooks, waitresses, and menials. The action is dispersed in a series of brief interludes embedded and almost immersed in the routine complexity of kitchen work. Each individual episode is severely curtailed in time and leaves little mark on its successors. There is only one major climax that must serve both phases of the play—Wesker does not call them "acts"—and this occurs when Peter, the most verbally articulate character, grabs a chopper, cuts through a gas main, and stops what for him is an intolerable routine. Then he rushes out and leaves the manager and others to sustain and rapidly contain the consequences of his action.

The play was of course criticized for its lack of dramatic construction; and its first professional production in London had to wait for the success of later plays by Wesker. But the playwright defended his innovations: "for Shakespeare the world may have been a stage," but for him "it was a kitchen," where men and women were imprisoned and dwarfed by a grueling routine, and where specifically human actions could not have development and climax and consequence. He had found a form for what he had seen and felt.

Wesker must then have read a book on "how to write a play," for his next two plays are more conformist, each with three acts and far fewer *dramatis personæ;* the passage of time is more usual, the settings are easily realizable in the three walls of a box set. In *Roots,* the most eloquent of all these early plays, a heroine dominates the action.

But with *Chips With Everything* Wesker returned to a broader theme and presented two more of his "worlds." One shows conscripts in the R.A.F. on the parade-ground, developing from ill-coordinated individuals into a "fine body of men," efficient and faceless at the passing-out ceremony. The other shows, in interspersed scenes, the same conscripts in their barracks, but now bringing their individual needs and affections to various, disconnected, and imperfect life; in these scenes Wesker shows another development towards a group-life, but far less certain or effective than that of the parade ground. When the recruits voluntarily follow a leader, the group reaction is efficient, and when they combine to protect and aid the unfortunate Smiler—the rejected and suffering fool—their corporate life becomes considerate. But at the end, these actions have no consequence; the random collection of individuals disperses as the airmen are posted to different stations.

With *Chips* and *The Kitchen,* Wesker was recognized as a social dramatist whose plays need large casts and are made effective by choreographic direction. But then his next play to be performed was *The Four Seasons,* which has only two characters and tells the story of a love affair. His director and the critics seemed quite unprepared for this: it was a new and unexpected development. But the love affair was private, intimate, and finally inconclusive: Wesker was magnifying one of the individualistic incidents of *The Kitchen* or *Chips,* artificially sustaining a confrontation (that in any of his ways of life is naturally tentative and impermanent) for as long as a symbolistic framework of Winter-Spring-Summer-Autumn would permit. His dialogue attempted to hold on to moments by the use of song or formal address, and so it suggests the antipathies, submissions, and cruelties at the heart of short moments of apparent concord.

With *Their Very Own and Golden City,* which is his last play to be performed (though most of it was written before *The Four Seasons*), Wesker once more used the wide scene, only less restricted in time, place, and type of character. Here is the whole life of a working-class boy becoming a famous Town Planner, knighted for his services. Like *The Four Seasons* it did not please the critics: flashbacks in the last scenes from middle-age to youth (involving two actors for a single character); a setting that has to change during the action (especially in the last eleven scenes, where Wesker wants to have the progression of a film rather than of a play); the obvious propagandist and autobiographical elements combined with the compression of characters to types that was necessary in order to contain such wide-ranging subject matter within bounds of a three-hour performance—all this gave offense. If Wesker had been content with his own earlier dramatic forms he would have been in less danger of being judged a failure. But a more demanding form is what he seeks—in order to present the themes he has always considered significant. He is using the theater to explore, to demonstrate in more comprehensive and more subtle ways: that is why he is a dramatist before he is a propagandist.

Although the new British dramatists do not want to make statements or define their aims, they are creatively involved with society and seek a full revelation in their plays of what they find in the worlds around them and within them. They write for the theater because this is the art form which allows them to show the complexity of those worlds: the permanent and frightening forces that lie behind each explosive crisis and each boring, dehumanizing routine; the limitations, dangers, and excitements of a personal, subjective view; the impossibility of judging any man except in relation to others; the strength of truth and permanence of idealism. They write youthful, topical, sensational, theatrical plays because the theatre can be a realistic, exploratory, complicated and, hence, responsible medium. They are promising and already important dramatists.

The Early Fifties

by John Russell Taylor

With practically any 'overnight revolution' it turns out, when one comes to look more closely, that the signs were there to be read by anyone with enough foresight and that the revolution proper was only the final culmination of a whole string of minor skirmishes with whatever party happened to be in control at the time. Was this the case in the British theatre in the years before Osborne? Let us see.

At this distance of time it is difficult to recapture the flavour of that now remote era, but perhaps the best way to begin is to take a look at what was happening in London during the previous year. As usual, most of the big critical successes—those which were felt to add appreciably to the cultural life of the city—were foreign. It was, you will recall, Ugo Betti year, when after a belated discovery by the Third Programme he emerged in the West End with three plays, *The Burnt Flowerbed, The Queen and the Rebels,* and *Summertime.* There were also *The Waltz of the Toreadors* (Anouilh), *The Count of Clerembard* (Aymé), *Hotel Paradiso* (Feydeau), *Nina* (Roussin), *The Strong are Lonely* (Hochwalder), *The Threepenny Opera* (Brecht)—and *Waiting for Godot,* which surprised everyone by going on from the Arts to become a commercial as well as a critical success. (Ionesco also appeared unobtrusively in February 1955, when *The Lesson* was a little-noticed curtain-raiser at the Arts, but his real impact was delayed until the coupling there of *The Bald Prima Donna* and *The New Tenant* in November 1956.) America, equally as usual, contributed a sizeable portion of our theatrical

"The Early Fifties," by John Russell Taylor. From *Anger and After: A Guide to the New British Drama* (London: Methuen & Co. Ltd., 1962); also published as *The Angry Theater* (New York: Hill & Wang, Inc., 1962).

fare with musicals (*Plain and Fancy, The Pajama Game*) and straight plays of various sorts (*Anniversary Waltz, Gigi, The Good Sailor, The Rainmaker*).

From British authors, there were an unusual number of artless musicals; in addition to *The Boy Friend* and *Salad Days,* which ran throughout the year, there were another Sandy Wilson *The Buccaneer, A Girl called Jo, Romance in Candlelight, She Smiled at Me, Summer Song, Twenty Minutes South, The Water Gipsies, Wild Grows the Heather,* and *Wild Thyme;* there were also a number of forgotten light comedies and thrillers, one of which, *The House by the Lake,* starring Flora Robson, was one of the year's big hits. But what was there which might be supposed to enhance the reputation of the British theatre? Well, there were a couple of good revivals (Frankie Howerd in *Charley's Aunt,* a glittering *Misalliance* from H. M. Tennent) and three notable seasons: the Gielgud-Ashcroft season at the Palace (*King Lear* and *Much Ado*), John Clements at the Saville (*The Wild Duck, The Rivals* and a capable new political drama, Norman King's *The Shadow of Doubt*), and the Brook-Scofield season at the Phoenix, which offered memorable productions of *The Family Reunion, Hamlet* and one new play, *The Power and the Glory,* which turned out to be Pierre Bost's French version of Greene's novel Englished by Denis Cannan. But at least Cannan, since *Captain Carvallo,* had been a name to conjure with; he was 'promising' and certainly a ray of hope on the dim theatrical scene. Otherwise it could hardly be said that new drama had much to offer. Two veterans were seen off form, Coward with *South Sea Bubble* and Priestley with *Mr Kettle and Mrs Moon.* Rattigan, the reigning king of the English stage, had *Separate Tables* still running from the previous year, and another 'veteran', Gerald Savory, scored a mild success with a slightly Chekhovian comedy *A Likely Tale.* Of the 'post-war' playwrights, few as they were, only one, Peter Ustinov, had a play staged, *Romanoff and Juliet,* which though far from his best proved a big success. Fry, the great reviver of that verse drama which people had been expecting to save the theatre for the previous ten years or so, had been silent since *The Dark is Light Enough* in the previous year, and would remain so, translations apart, until *Curtmantle* in 1961. The same almost exactly was true of John Whiting, centre of controversy since his *Saint's Day* won the Arts Council prize in 1951: his *Marching Song* of 1954 had achieved no great success with the public, although some critics liked it, and apart from a couple of television scripts and an abortive out-of-town tour he eschewed drama until *The Devils* seven years later. The only decisive success of the year on every level, in fact, was almost the most anachronistic play of them all, the novelist Enid Bagnold's glittering and artificial high comedy *The Chalk Garden,* which could have been written almost unaltered at any time since Wilde.

And was this really all? To all intents and purposes, yes. A new surrealistic revue, *Cranks,* by the choreographer John Cranko seemed to presage a breakaway from the genre's routine theatrical parish-pumpery. A new manager called Michael Codron put on a comedy called *Send for Catty,* but it would have taken quite abnormal prescience to recognize here the future impresario of Mortimer and Pinter. A small and struggling company, Theatre Workshop, which had hitherto concentrated mainly on classical revivals and occasional didactic political pieces, achieved the first West End transfer from their East London home, the Theatre Royal, Stratford, with *The Good Soldier Schweik,* dramatized by Ewan MacColl from Hašek. And in April 1956 a new group, the English Stage Company, took over the Royal Court Theatre with the avowed intention of putting on new plays in repertory. Their first production, *The Mulberry Bush,* by the novelist Angus Wilson, had, in fact, been previously produced in Bristol, and though it got mixed notices it was generally agreed to be interesting and enterprising. Their second was a superior Broadway hit, Arthur Miller's *The Crucible.* And their third was *Look Back in Anger,* which opened just over a month after the management had been installed.

But before this happened one would have been quite justified in regarding the year as something very much like the end of an era. One by one the theatre clubs and brave little try-out theatres were closing (the New Watergate, the New Lindsey, the Boltons, the Q) and only the Arts remained with sufficient facilities to do justice to a difficult new work, when it could find one (*Waiting for Godot* and *The Waltz of the Toreadors* began at the Arts; the only new native play was a rather precious and high-flown poetic drama, *Darkling Child,* by W. S. Merwin and Dido Milroy). But finding new drama of sufficient interest was the main problem, and though new plays by new playwrights did emerge quite frequently, the main defence offered for British drama when it was compared (unfavourably, of course) with what was being produced in America, France, and elsewhere was that really Rattigan had shown himself in *The Browning Version* and *The Deep Blue Sea* to be a major international dramatist and it was only native British modesty which prevented us from realizing the fact. Even the most enthusiastic defenders of this view, however, could not deny that exciting new dramatists had been rather thin on the ground since Rattigan. There had been the post-war revival of poetic drama, led by Christopher Fry, who after a couple of pre-war religious pieces scored a surprise success with *A Phoenix Too Frequent* in 1946 and especially *The Lady's Not For Burning* (1948) and proceeded with a sequence of seasonal plays (*Venus Observed,* 1950, and *The Dark is Light Enough,* 1954) to show that verse drama could be good box-office as well (naturally, the presence of such luminaries as John Gielgud, Laurence Olivier, and Edith Evans in his casts did not harm the plays' chances at all either). But apart from the unexpected reappearance of T. S. Eliot in the London theatre with *The Cocktail Party* (1949) and *The Confidential Clerk* (1953), Fry's championship of poetry in the theatre went more or less unsupported, the appeal of other verse dramatists proving either merely modish (Ronald Duncan's *This Way to the Tomb*) or too parochial (Norman Nicholson's *Old Man of the Mountains;* Anne Ridler's *The Shadow Factory*) and soon most practitioners of verse drama betook themselves to the radio, where Louis MacNeice in particular had outstanding success with such plays as *The Dark Tower, Christopher Columbus* and *The Queen of Air and Darkness.*

And since this particular revival had fizzled out there had been very little. There was Peter Ustinov, of course, who had been 'promising' since *House of Regrets* in 1942 (when he was twenty-one) and after a sequence of eccentric and personal half-successes like *Blow Your Own Trumpet, The Banbury Nose,* and *The Indifferent Shepherd,* had at last achieved a solid success with his satirical comedy *The Love of Four Colonels* (1951), which confirmed critics in the idea that one of these days he might at last produce an unmistakable masterpiece; unfortunately they hoped for a 'serious' masterpiece, while his more serious pieces—*The Moment of Truth, The Empty Chair*—seemed mainly to confirm that his real talent was for grotesque comedy. But at least *Romanoff and Juliet* revived hopes for him; hopes, alas, which despite *Paris Not So Gay* have not yet been justified.

Then there were a couple of older writers who really came to theatrical prominence only in the fifties: Graham Greene, for instance, whose first play, *The Living Room* (1953), though offering nothing very new to readers of his novels, did prove something of a sensation in a West End theatre starved of ideas (rather as his original film script *The Third Man* had done in the British cinema), and who has continued to demonstrate a satisfactory grasp of the playwright's craft in *The Potting Shed* and *The Complaisant Lover*. Another was N. C. Hunter, whose earliest play had been produced as long before as 1934, but who first became a name to reckon with when his *Waters of the Moon* was taken up as a suitable prestige production for Festival year (1951) and packed with stars, headed by Edith Evans and Sybil Thorndike. The same almost inevitable success attended his second play staged in similar circumstances, *A Day by the Sea,* with John Gielgud, Ralph Richardson, and Sybil Thorndike, and his third, *A Touch of the Sun,* with Michael Redgrave and Diana Wynyard. The unkind said that nothing could fail with such casts (an assertion recently disproved by Enid Bagnold's *The Last Joke,* which ran barely six weeks despite the presence in its cast of Gielgud and Richardson); the kind said that because of the casts assembled the plays themselves had received too little attention. The truth, as usual, is betwixt and between: Hunter's plays are as well put together as any in the English theatre, with good meaty acting parts, lively, literate dialogue and a real feeling for atmosphere of a tenuous sub-Chekhovian nature (resembling Chekhov, that is, as usually misunderstood by British actors and directors). They even, particularly *A Touch of the Sun,* have their moments of original observation, but basically they are the work of a solid, academic dramatist, and that, though not a little, is perhaps not quite enough.

Now, who does that leave us? On the stage, at least, no one very much except Denis Cannan and John Whiting (the proviso 'on the stage' is necessary, as we shall see later). Denis Cannan (born 1919) has only once, with *Captain Carvallo* in 1950, obtained a success commensurate with his obvious talents, and the reason for this is not too difficult to see: since his first play *Max,* an uncharacteristic stab at intense drama on the subject of conflicting ideologies, he has concentrated, not on comedy of ideas, which is a recognized if chancy English form, but on intelligent farce, which to most British playgoers sounds like a contradiction in terms. *Captain Carvallo* itself is almost as much comedy as it is farce, and therefore more acceptable than the rest, particularly as it introduces a note of seriousness at the end after its witty variations on the theme of the victor wooing the vanquished in the shape of their prettier womenfolk. The theme again is, of course, the conflict of ideologies, and the close thematic relationship between *Max* and *Captain Carvallo,* in fact, serves to underline the principle behind most of Cannan's work—one particularly hard for London playgoers to swallow in practice—that tragedy and farce are merely different sides of the same medal. The theme of conflicting ideologies as material for farce recurs in *Misery Me!,* which is based on one of the principal balances in ordinary life—the balance between two sworn enemies which gives meaning to their lives and would be destroyed if either were removed—and on an inquiry concerning the nature and durability of love. The matter was found too weighty for its framework and the play survived barely three weeks in London.

In his two later plays Cannan appears to have learnt the lesson, since in neither *You and Your Wife* nor *Who's Your Father?* is there much suggestion of a 'message'. The first makes two dissentient married couples (one husband is about to run off with the other's wife) try to sort out their problems while held in captivity by a couple of improbable gangsters, and the second involves a snobbish *nouveau-riche* couple in all sorts of agonizing complications when their daughter's irresponsible fiancé poses as a genealogist and offers them some pretty disreputable antecedents, so that when a bishop turns up to claim the father as his long-lost son he is understandably mistaken for a white-slaver and bribed to leave the country. Neither has any great pretensions to penetration of character (never Cannan's strong point); instead they manoeuvre their puppet-characters through a series of intricately devised comic situations more in the manner of a latter-day Feydeau. Consequently their sophisticated agility mystified the sort of audience who might approve of basic farce at the Whitehall, while audiences who might have enjoyed them were put off by never quite knowing whether they were supposed to be taken seriously or not. However, audiences are becoming less and less inclined to demand such unequivocal indications from their playwrights, and Denis Cannan may yet come into his own.

John Whiting (born 1915) is a more complex case: his arrival was more spectacular and his subsequent withdrawal from the theatre more complete, and while Denis Cannan did not make his initial impact specifically as something new in the theatre, Whiting decidedly did. He began as an actor after a period at R.A.D.A., and continued to act after being demobbed in 1945. His first play, *Conditions of Agreement,* was written shortly after the war, and was put away to be rewritten later for television as *A Walk in the Desert,* of which Whiting subsequently remarked: 'The critics said "What on earth is he doing? He's forty something and he's writing like a twenty-eight year old." They were dead right, of course. I changed a good deal, but I couldn't get away from the basic thing.' His next play, *Saint's Day* (1947-49), was also put away unproduced for a while, and then he wrote *A Penny for a Song,* a fantastic poetic comedy (in prose, although one or two critics tried to enrol him among Fry's followers on the strength of it) about two Dorset eccentrics, one a blustering would-be strategist, the other a gentle fire-fighter, at the time of the Napoleonic Wars. This was actually his first play to be staged (in 1951) and though not particularly successful commercially it marked him as certainly a writer to watch. Some six months later the earlier *Saint's Day* was picked as one of the three finalists in the Arts Councils Festival of Britain Play Competition, was produced at the Arts to the general incomprehension of critics and public, and then, amid a storm of protest, awarded the prize.

If one looks again at *Saint's Day* now it is very difficult to understand why it should have caused all this fuss—certainly it is no more exotic or obscure than many of the television plays which are now accepted without demur. But then *The Times* drama critic found it 'of a badness that must be called indescribable' and provoked a correspondence in the course of which Tyrone Guthrie and Peter Brook called it 'remarkable' and found 'its passion and its unbroken tension . . . the products of a new and extraordinary theatrical mind', while Peggy Ashcroft and John Gielgud called it 'moving, beautiful, and fascinating'. Both sides in the dispute seem in retrospect to exaggerate. The play, which takes as its theme one of perennial fascination to Whiting, self-destruction, is visibly immature, overloaded with literary and philosophical reference and playing its plot (which concerns an old writer obsessed with the idea that people are plotting to kill him who, with the other members of his household and a visiting critic, is swept into a series of violent actions skirting if not toppling into melodrama and ending in a number of violent deaths) for considerably more than it is worth. It is rather pretentious in conception, sometimes absurd, and yet at the same time it does generate a powerful theatrical excitement if one allows oneself to be carried away by the momentum of the piece and not ask too many awkward questions.

The third play in this group, *Marching Song* (1954), again takes up the theme of self-destruction: it concerns the dilemma of a general offered the choice of suicide or a trial and public disgrace. Feeling he has nothing to live for, he is about to commit suicide, as the Chancellor wants, when he is distracted by a young girl who restores to him the will to live. Should he choose to live, at any cost? To decide this he must explore his own motives, his own pride, and his discovery of a flaw in that pride (he lost a battle because he refused to plough his tanks through a mass of children to victory, for once putting humanity before his pride in military achievement), before he can choose, quite calmly, to die. This emerged as Whiting's most balanced and artistically successful play to date, eloquently written and creating its dramatic tensions very cunningly, even though almost all the action is internal rather than external. (For this reason Whiting calls it 'an anti-theatrical play'.) It is distinguished, it is formidably intelligent, and yet somehow it is all just a little cold and lifeless, just as *Saint's Day* was over-literary and allusive and *A Penny for a Song,* despite its charm and invention, a little lacking in real impetus and *élan*. Their qualities, in a word, are such as could give great pleasure to a properly conditioned audience, but could never hope to take an unprepared audience by storm.

It is significant, in this connexion, to compare the reception of the earlier play with that of *The Devils* in 1961, when Whiting returned to the London theatre after a seven-year silence—a voluntary withdrawal, it seems, during which he worked on film scripts, wrote a bitter comedy, *The Gates of Summer* (1956), which never reached London, and one short and insignificant television thriller, *Eye Witness.* In *The Devils,* which draws its subject from Aldous Huxley's book *"The Devils of Loudun,* we find precisely the same qualities as in *Marching Song:* great skill in marshalling the material, great intelligence in its analysis and recreation in dramatic terms, and a remarkable flair for eloquent dialogue which only lets the author down (as it let Shaw down at a similar point in *St John*) when a great emotional profession of faith is needed beyond the scope of cool, intelligent appraisal. But with all its skill and intelligence the play lacks something: in particular the choice of the rather ordinary libertine priest Grandier rather than the possessed nun, Soeur Jeanne des Anges, his chief tormentor, as the central figure seems a mistake, especially as it involves simplifying the motives of the nuns (who are made conscious deceivers over their supposed diabolical possession instead of self-deluding neurotics) to the point where they become not only tiresomely commonplace but in the historical context totally incredible. The choice of Grandier as centrepiece is obviously deliberate (again, the theme is self-destruction) and the re-distribution of dramatic emphasis consequent upon it is deliberate, but that does not prevent one thinking it basically wrong, since it makes the material seem that much less interesting than intrinsically it is. But nevertheless *The Devils* has been hailed as a masterpiece, or nearly, by most of the critics, and has achieved a considerable success with the public where Whiting's earlier plays flopped ignominiously. *The Devils* was obviously a happy first choice for commission by the recently established London branch of the Stratford Memorial Theatre company, and Whiting has been commissioned to write them another. He has also completed an enigmatic one-acter *No Why,* involving (again) a suicide, this time a child's. The audience is now conditioned, and Whiting, honourable precursor of the new drama, has reappeared at last to ride on the wave of its success.

So that was the London theatre between the Festival and *Look Back in Anger*. Television was still finding its feet, and there is nothing much to be looked for there (indeed, the independent network, from which most of the more exciting television drama has come, did not begin operations, even on a very restricted basis, until September 1955). Radio was rather better, and indeed in general the Third Programme proves the brightest spot in a depressing picture: two dramatists in particular, Henry Reed, known to the stage only for his translations of Betti, and Giles Cooper, who gravitated to radio after having a play, *Never Get Out,* produced at the Gateway in 1950 (and later at the Arts), ventured boldly into new territory which would in those days have yielded very little in the way of possibilities for the commercial stage. Reed's work is often nearer the 'feature' than drama proper, as in programmes like the autobiographical *Return to Naples* and the impressionistic *Streets of Pompeii;* sometimes, indeed, as in his brilliant series on Herbert Reeve, Hilda Tablett, General Gland, and the rest (a saga begun with *A Very Great Man Indeed*), it is inspired spoofing of the feature.

Giles Cooper (born 1918) is more relevant to our purpose, however, since all his best works are very definitely 'plays', even though some of them are so conceived as to be virtually unthinkable in terms of any medium but radio. From *Never Get Out,* an elusive duologue between an army deserter and a disconsolate woman with a death wish set in a house supposedly about to be bombed, Cooper has specialized in the exploration of strange emotional states in the margin of human experience, sometimes with strongly macabre overtones and generally on the surface at least in terms of comedy. A whole series of progressively more experimental plays culminated in *Mathry Beacon* (1956), a composite picture of the lives of a group of soldiers looking after a deflector hidden away in the Welsh mountains. His characteristic sinister-comic mode has subsequently been seen to advantage in such fantasies as *Unman, Wittering and Zigo,* an obsessive tale of a teacher's persecution by his pupils; *Part of the View,* in which a Nigerian governess takes a roundabout revenge on her English employers for their condescension and ironically thereby saves their marriage; *Before the Monday,* in which an innocent and a would-be suicide gradually change places; *Without the Grail,* about mysterious happenings in a mad planter's private kingdom in the Assam hills, and *The Return of General Forefinger,* in which the desire of a general's widow to recover all the statues of her husband scattered round the world is met by a sculptor who secretly makes them himself (the list of plot-situations is wearisome, but it does give some idea of his range). One or two of these, like *Mathry Beacon,* would not work anywhere but on radio; others, like *Before the Monday* and *Without the Grail,* are quite conceivable in stage terms if properly adapted, as *Without the Grail* was by Cooper himself for television. There seemed, in fact, no intrinsic reason by 1960 why Cooper should not, if he so desired, turn his attentions successfully to the stage which in 1950 had clearly not been ready for him, and now, finally, he is about to do so with a new play, *Everything in the Garden.* With his extraordinary skill in the invention of lively, expressive dialogue and unexpected but telling dramatic situations he should rapidly prove to be a considerable acquisition.

But even in spite of Whiting, Cannan, and Cooper (most of whose work dates in any case from after the advent of the 'new drama'), the outlook for the young dramatist must have looked fairly grim around the beginning of 1956. There was hardly a straw in the wind, since it would have been an optimist indeed who relied too strongly on the English Stage Company or Theatre Workshop to save the day. Anyway, managers and critics would ask each other periodically, where was the new dramatic talent to be found? And what sort of reception would the public give it if and when it did emerge?—none too enthusiastic if the experience of Whiting and Cannan was anything to go by. Then, on 8 May 1956 came the revolution. . . .

New English Drama

by Raymond Williams

England may be slow and tired in other ways, but in writing its literary history it is very quick off the mark. A movement can be announced, and a book written about it, on the basis of two or three works by comparatively young writers. Inevitably, as this movement develops, its members are seen more clearly as themselves, and the simple original version cannot be maintained. This discourages nobody, for the movement is then seen to have divided into movements, and the whole process begins again.

In recent English drama this has been particularly noticeable. Of course there is always some justification for it, as new emphases appear. But the turnover has been so rapid that if we attempt to keep up with it by 'movements' we shall simply run ourselves into the ground. My own impression of the last six or seven years of English drama is of a period of extreme confusion and eclecticism, made more so by a genuine burst of vitality and energy. I do not think we can begin to understand this period unless we put it in the context of the general development of drama in this century.

The first general factor is that for seventy years, in England, we have had a split drama. Even though the theatre as a whole has served only a minority of the people, there has been a clear division within this minority. The division goes back to a critical period in European culture, beginning in the last generation of the last century. At this time, in many fields of art and thought, a minority of the dominant middle class broke away from its own class habits. There had been individual breaks before, but now the break was substantial enough to emerge in new institutions: the 'free' or 'independent' theatres which spread across Europe and reached England in 1892. Ever since that time, the development of drama as an art has been in the hands of the free theatres. Their work has only ever been a small percentage of the plays actually written and acted, but with rare exceptions it has been the only work that can be taken at all seriously beyond its own place and generation.

The free theatres, however, have always been weak. It has been rare, in England, for any to last more than a few seasons. The majority theatre has been reasonably prosperous, and, since it is normally quite uncreative, it has taken over, as part of its programme, any work the free theatres have established. This has meant the spread of goods plays, but usually it has also deprived the free theatres of the chance of any consistent long-term development. A principal reason for the general appearance of eclecticism, and for the extreme rapidity of successive fashions, has been this state of affairs in the institutions.

The middle-class drama which began in the eighteenth century has its own orthodox forms, which have continued to serve the majority theatre. These are, principally, spectacle, melodrama and farce, on one side of the line; sentimental comedy and domestic intrigue on the other. No play of any consequence has come from these kinds. But there were also two other forms, with a mixed history: domestic realism and romantic drama. The latter has roots as far back as the Renaissance; the former is a distinctively new middle-class form. At the time of the break, in the last quarter of the nineteenth century, it was these two forms which were developed by the free theatres. Each found its highest point in Ibsen, who remains of commanding importance. Each has continued to be important in the free theatres down to our own time.

The break was in part a break towards realism: a revolt against orthodox middle-class drama in its own best terms. The central statement of this revolt was and is quite simple: that what passes for realistic drama is in fact telling lies—it is not about real people in real situations, but about conventional characters (superficial and flattering) in conventional situations (theatrical and unreal). Each phase of this revolt has seen the same complaint against the stilted, old-fashioned conventions of the majority theatre, and the same kind of counter-offensive: an aggressive thrusting of new people, new problems, new ideas into the centre of the stage. The revolt has many major plays to its credit, from *Ghosts* to *A View from the Bridge*. But, typically, it has been the injection of new content into an orthodox dramatic form. This has meant, quite naturally, that new drama, of this sort, has been discussed almost exclusively in terms of its new content.

Yet the break was not only of this kind. In the last seventy years, in the free theatres, we have seen a greater invention of new dramatic forms than in any previous period. The terms invented to describe these new forms have varied considerably. Between expressionism, symbolism, epic theatre, contemporary verse drama, and anti-theatre there has, in fact, been a good deal of overlapping. It is possible to sort them out, around the work of particular dramatists, but it is really more important to see what they have in common. This, above all, is the rejection of the versions of dramatic reality made habitual by the middle-class drama. The complaint is not now that the plays in the majority theatre are not realistic enough: not about significant people and problems. The complaint is that the starting-point, in such plays, is quite wrong. The orthodox drama, it is argued, starts and ends in appearances. It is concerned to put on the stage a real-looking room, real-looking people making real-sounding conversation. This is all right, as far as it goes, but inevitably it is not far. The whole world of inner and normally inarticulate experience, the whole world of social process, which makes history yet is never clearly present on the surface, are alike excluded. The more real it all looks, the less real it may actually be.

This judgment has been made from very widely differing positions. It has been made by Christians and Platonists, convinced that behind apparent reality is a greater and more decisive spiritual reality. It has been made by men influenced by new kinds of philosophy and psychology, convinced, for different reasons, that the surface of life is often deceptive, and that to touch reality it is necessary to penetrate this surface. It has been made, finally, by social revolutionaries, concerned with the difference between the superstructure of life and its deeper structure, and between false consciousness and real consciousness. From all these varying positions, the assault on what has come to be called 'naturalist' drama has been mounted. All are agreed that a dramatic form which simply reproduces the surface, however faithfully, is of little use. Differences appear, inevitably, when the new starting-point is taken, but in dramatic method there is at least a family likeness in most of these new kinds. The action, scene and persons of the play have, in varying degrees, a deliberate unfamiliarity of surface. The intention is to break through conventions and appearances to the underlying reality, or, put another way, to use new kinds of dramatic effect which will communicate this underlying reality to the audience. There is some overlapping, here, with the more developed forms of the 'new realism', which, while retaining the familiar surface, uses particular devices to allow the underlying reality to break through at points of crisis. Thus, alongside the majority drama which continues with the old forms unchanged, we have a wide range of work, its categories continually blurring from the new realism using new methods at points of crisis, through the realistic verse drama, to the more extreme forms of full symbolism and expressionism.

This, in our own generation, is our confused inheritance. But in fact it was only in the 1950s that the effects of the whole range became active in England. There had been isolated uses of expressionism, by Sean O'Casey in the 1920s, and by Auden and Isherwood in the 1930s. But in those days it was always called 'German expressionism', which by definition would not grow in English soil. The main English contribution to the general movement was in the development of new kinds of verse drama. Until the early 1950s, this seemed to be the most promising line, and it is worth looking back, briefly, to see why this was so and why, in the end, it petered out.

The verse drama was a movement of writers, rather than of men closely involved with the theatre. This was inevitable, since the links between literature and the theatre had been tenuous or nonexistent for generations. The point seized by the verse dramatists was the question of dramatic speech. It was not possible, they argued, to express anything like full human experience by the imitation of probable conversation. Only if the dramatist recovered his full powers of expression, rather than allowing himself to be limited by the probable expressive powers of his characters, could the full range of human experience return to the drama. In its early stages, the revival of verse drama was closely involved with a search for new kinds of dramatic action, as in Yeats's 'plays for dancers' and Eliot's unfinished *Sweeney Agonistes.* But because there was no permanent theatre in which these experiments could be followed through, the search was very difficult. Eliot achieved one major success, in *Murder in the Cathedral,* where he could draw on the church as an active body of ritual and formal language. When he turned to contemporary action, however, his plays ran into major difficulties. There is a steady abandonment, from *The Family Reunion* to *The Elder Statesman,* of any attempt to create non-realistic dramatic action. Ironically, there is also a steady abandonment of any attempt to use dramatic verse for its original purposes: to express the full range of experience rather than the version of experience that could be reasonably put into the mouths of probable characters. The two kinds of change are connected. It proved impossible to write dramatic verse of any intensity while the ordinary dramatic action of naturalism was retained. It is asking too much of any actor to speak verse of some intensity while answering the telephone, returning an umbrella, or pouring drinks. But the telephone, the umbrella and the drinks were not there for the purposes of the drama. They were there, on naturalist principles, to persuade audiences that this was a probable action. What had originally been a powerful extension of drama, into new areas of human action and speech, declined to a mannerism. It did not really matter whether *The Elder Statesman* was in verse or not, since the original attempt at a new kind of drama had in any case been abandoned. The existence of the majority theatre, complacent as always in its conventional wisdom, had dragged down this whole venture to its own size.

The verse drama of Christopher Fry had never represented so real a challenge. Its weakness always was its tendency to use verse to decorate a romantic action, rather than to touch new dramatic experience. When it was taken up, by the majority theatre, this tendency ran wild: the writing became almost purely atmospheric —'poetic' in a bad old sense—while even the romantic drama at its base became suspiciously like straight costume drama. Meanwhile, the disappearance of the Left-wing theatre of the 1930s, which had used verse drama successfully, left an identification of the verse-play with one doctrine only: a particular kind of Christianity. Coming on top of its technical difficulties, this doctrinal isolation was too much for it. It was very exposed, and was easily attacked. It disappeared from the theatre into broadcasting, where it retained some vitality because the problem of action was less acute. But even there it retained some of the crippling marks of its minority identification. When people thought of English verse drama, now, they thought of religious or quasi-religious themes, or of fragments from a classical education, all declined into mannerism.

The serious verse drama was gone before the two major influences that were to replace it had properly appeared. The first influence was the reopening of the English theatre to the full range of European practice. The work of Anouilh, Sartre, Brecht, Beckett, Giraudoux, Ionesco came as a revelation, especially since people were feeling that elsewhere only mannerism and the commercial theatre were left. Much of this work realized, in practice, what the revival of verse drama had originally been about: the expansion of dramatic action and speech to a more vital and more extended human range. Slowly, over the last seven or eight years, a number of English dramatists have absorbed these varied influences, and produced their own new kinds of work. In the long run, this is probably the decisive trend.

In the early stage of this readjustment, however, a quite different element appeared. This was a challenge of the kind already noted: one of those critical points at which the majority drama is challenged, not so much because of its form as because of its content. The same thing was happening in fiction, with a similar indifference to the more advanced kinds of technical experiment. What was wrong, it was widely felt and argued, was that the speech and action of the typical majority theatre were miles away from contemporary life. Instead of embodying the actual lives of possible audiences, the theatre was given over to theatrical versions of the pre-war rituals of middle-class life (pre-war sometimes meant, quite rightly, pre-1914). When this revolt at last broke through, it was very like the many that had preceded it. Its great virtue was new content, which came through with an evident excitement and vitality. Conspicuously it was the life and style of a new generation, as in Osborne's *Look Back in Anger*. This depended, characteristically, on an independent theatre, which held it just long enough, through the first critical stage, to enable it to get through to a wider audience. The effect of this breakthrough was a general release of energy, and the play itself was no more and no less than this: uncontrolled, unresolved but directly powerful. Shelagh Delaney's *A Taste of Honey* was similarly a direct revolt against the prevailing middle-class drama, and made its way through an independent theatre. Within a very short time there was a sense of a general movement.

This has been called the emergence of working-class drama, but the description is too general. On the whole the life that came through was that of people disorganized and drifting: youth and poverty were factors in this, but the general state of feeling mattered more than any precise social setting. Shelagh Delaney's play is probably the nearest to transcription of an actual way of living, but in its selection of characters and situations moves the emphasis on to disorganization. The young people in *Look Back in Anger* are probably actors rather than the ambiguous social types they were claimed to be, and in *The Entertainer* this particular opportunity for stressing mobility, restlessness and disorganization was directly taken. John Arden's *Live Like Pigs* centres directly on a mobile, restless, vagrant family. A good deal of social experience was expressed through these plays, but not much of it was that of the actual working class. This matters only as a point against the ordinary simplification. The true social experience that was coming through was that of a general restlessness, disorganization and frustration, and expression of these moods was simpler through the selection of especially restless and disorganized people. The plays are an indifferent guide to the generality of English social life, of which they were often taken to be an expression. Much more they are an expression of a structure of feeling which was quite widely operative. This explains why they were largely played to and welcomed by young and minority middle-class audiences, where this structure of feeling was most explicit.

Behind these valuable plays came a wave of conscious and fashionable 'low-life' drama, in which crooks and prostitutes were the natural characters. The situation has many points of resemblance with that of Germany in the 1920s, when Brecht expressed similar feeling through similar means, notably in *The Threepenny Opera.* The one area of actual social life which has found direct dramatic expression has been that of the Jewish East End, in the work of Arnold Wesker and Bernard Kops. This had qualities of vitality and expressiveness which made it dramatically easier to handle, but it is not quite the exception it appears, for again it is in part the drama of an inherently mobile minority, and the sense of disorganization, restlessness and frustration comes very powerfully through Wesker's plays. Behan used a particular facet of Irish life in the same way, in *The Hostage,* which is interesting not so much as a continuation of the Irish drama which in Synge and O'Casey has been so important in this century, but as a contrast with it. *The Hostage* is not so much an Irish scene as a microcosm of disorganization and restlessness; more like Wesker's *The Kitchen* than like O'Casey.

What came through, then, was not so much a new area of life, in the ordinary descriptive sense, as a new wave of feeling. In fact it had some elements in common with the drama it evidently replaced; in Eliot and Fry, also, the dominating themes had been restlessness and loss of direction. But these were now expressed in new voices, and with a different edge. In the late plays of Eliot, and in the conscious atmosphere of Fry, there had been a sense of indulgence in these emotional states, for their own sake. There was again indulgence, in several of the new plays, but in the best of them there was a new sound: that of ordinary human voices trying to live through the despair. This is perhaps at its most effective in *A Taste of Honey,* where, almost without artifice, the language of care and love keeps counterpointing the convincing bitterness, and where the play ends in a rooted disorder yet one through which a new life is coming and is given a blessing. The idea of a new life, in a more generalized and consciously political way, comes clearly through Wesker, and the voice of the political aspiration is new in that it is presented primarily as the sudden articulation of individual energy.

What was first noticed, however, was the new edge: the bitter, almost inarticulate rage at the general condition. Dramatically, *Look Back in Anger* is mainly this kind of declaration, and the most effective points in Wesker's plays are declarations of the same kind. It is not a doctrine that is declared, as in Shaw or in Ibsen's *Enemy of the People*; it is a primarily emotional protest, barely articulate, with an intensity beyond its nominal causes. The cry was recognized, in this form, by its immediate audiences.

We have then the curious situation of a revival of naturalist drama which, when its structure of feeling is analysed, is only intermittently consistent with naturalism. This new work is less the drama of social description and probability than the drama of a state of mind. It has used naturalism, consciously or unconsciously, mainly as a means of expressing this state of mind. This is why it is so stupid to call it 'kitchen-sink drama', which is a phrase that could only have got currency in a state of dramatic ignorance. That kind of work is at least eighty years old (perhaps a fair period for a phrase to get through to some of our newspapers), and the new work is not at all like it. We have not had documentaries of youth and poverty, but a number of intensely personal cries in the dark: a lyrical and romantic drama turned bitter and almost hopeless; a set of blues rhythms rather than a set of social problem plays.

This is where the other new factor of the 1950s, the renewed contacts with European drama, is so important. Beckett, particularly in *Waiting for Godot* and *All that Fall,* fitted this mood exactly. I remember reading in the program of *Waiting for Godot* that I was a kind of documentary about a very interesting kind of French vagrant; the point is no more and no less sensible than descriptions of *A Taste of Honey, The Kitchen, Look Back in Anger* in similar pseudo-objective social terms. A kind of life, theatrically communicable, is used to express a state of mind, by Beckett as plainly as by our own young dramatists; though in Beckett much more powerfully, and with much greater skill. In the plays of Ionesco, this kind of action had been developed into a distinctly anti-realistic convention, to express, however, basically similar feelings. A play like Pinter's *The Dumb Waiter* reflects quite directly and identifiably the methods and even the rhythms of Beckett and Ionesco, yet it is not far in texture from the new naturalism of the other young dramatists.

In this confused situation, we need a clear sense of dramatic history and development. What looked at first like simple archaism, a throwback to naturalism, is not turning out that way at all. Perhaps even some of the dramatists have been misled, by descriptions of their work in terms of social content (and thence, by old formulas, of naturalism), even where it is clear that the driving force is quite different. There is an evident reaching beyond the resources of ordinary conversation, by the use of music, songs, speeches. The immediate tradition of formal verse drama has been thoroughly rejected, but the tensions which originally led to it have all reappeared. In forty years of experiment the formal verse drama had reached a high level of technical skill, though it had never solved the problems of action. The new drama of recent years, rejecting that particular tradition, has had to start all over again, and is often, inevitably, crude and unfinished in its actual writing. Contact with the wider European tradition has restored the possibility of a new and mature direction, with stylization of quite different kinds.

It is interesting that there has been a turn to historical themes, which at a similar point in the development of verse drama seemed to offer the most practical way forward. The problem of the resources of speech is less pressing, when the obligation to reproduce contemporary actuality is thus removed. Still, we must make distinctions about these uses of history. There is a kind of historical play—well exemplified by Bolt's *A Man for All Seasons*—which is really a kind of ante-dated naturalism: the characters talk and feel in the twentieth century, but for action and interest are based in the sixteenth. This is often a strong form, in part because of the external interest of its historical material. Overlapping with this, but in certain respects going into a new kind, is the play of romantic intrigue—well illustrated by Whiting's *The Devils*. Hence the external interest is again evident, but the opportunity is taken—as only incidentally in historical naturalism—to create new kinds of theatrical effect: the colour and excitement of costume, the patterns of old rituals, the exhibition of torture and possession. Fry made romantic comedies out of this kind of material; Whiting has made a psychological drama. It has great theatrical attraction, because of its colour and movement, and it can usually be effectively produced and played, because it can draw directly on the methods of acting and producing Shakespeare (as distinct from Shakespeare's own dramatic methods, where all these elements are directed by the verse).

Again overlapping with this, but in certain respects going beyond it into a new kind, is the historical play which Brecht has taught us to call 'epic drama'. The point here is that while external historical interest is sometimes used (as in *Galileo*), and while full opportunity is often taken of theatrical colour and movement (as in *The Caucasian Chalk Circle*), the centre of the play is quite different; its primary interest is in a definition of meaning, belonging more to the present than to the past, which the action is quite consciously used to act out. It may be that Osborne's *Luther* is of this kind. Another example is Arden's *Serjeant Musgrave's Dance,* deliberately not located in any precise history, though consciously using its opportunities for theatrical colour and action, and centred in an examination of the meaning of violence, using the action as an image.

What we have then is not, in any textbook sense, a movement, with common aims and methods. We are in a confused and eclectic phase, which has valuably caught up elements of our own immediate tensions (the particular and recognizable tensions of Britain in the late 1950s and early 1960s) but which belongs, finally, to the period of European dramatic experiment which began more than eighty years ago. We are now taking part in this again, with exceptional energy, through an unusually strong generation of young dramatists who have turned to the theatre as a primary form. We have one new advantage: that in the performance of recent European drama, and from direct observation and contact with it, our producers, actors and audiences are much better equipped for experiment than in the period when the verse drama revival was beginning. Solid naturalist habits need not drag this generation back in the same way.

Yet also we have one continuing disadvantage: the split theatre. The minority theatres will continue to be the main channels of this work, but while they are financially insecure, and consequently subject all the time to the pressures of the commercial theatre, it will be difficult for any experiment to get enough time and resources for it to be properly carried through. Nothing is now more urgent than the creation of securely based professional companies, with real guarantees for their future, to carry forward, in several different ways, the possibilities now sensed. The weaknesses of our new drama are realized nowhere more clearly than among those working in it, and the confusion is not easy to bear when the practical opportunities to work through it are not easy to come by.

When the tradition is understood it can be excitingly extended, if it is given the opportunities which the energies and talents of this new dramatic generation seem to me to deserve.

The Hidden Face of Violence

by Tom Milne

". . . of a badness that must be called indescribable."

The Times on John Whiting's *Saint's Day.*

"A masterpiece of meaningless significance."

Punch on Harold Pinter's *The Birthday Party.*

"Another frightful ordeal."

The Sunday Times on John Arden's *Serjeant Musgrave's Dance.*

It is surely no accident that on the occasion of the first production of these three plays—*Saint's Day* in 1951, *The Birthday Party* in 1958, and *Serjeant Musgrave's Dance* in 1959—the virulence of the critics' attack was matched only by the vehemence of the underground support. Letters to the Press, denunciations of critical imbecility, protest, fury, frustration. The public, by and large, remained baffled and indifferent, and each of the plays closed after a minimum run. Yet, none of them has drifted into limbo. *Saint's Day* is still very much alive and kicking. *The Birthday Party* turns up in production all over the place, and is shortly to be seen on commercial television. It seems certain that the same thing will happen to *Serjeant Musgrave's Dance.*

In the case of John Whiting's play, dropped eight years ago into a theatre which measured its seriousness against a yardstick of Christopher Fry and T. S. Eliot, critical disfavour was to be expected. For the other two plays, appearing in the full flood of a theatre of social protest—where Osborne, Delaney, Behan and Wesker are hailed by all and sundry, and Joan Littlewood, after fourteen years of eye-opening work, is at last noticed—it is a little more surprising. For these three plays *are* social plays; not in the sense that they show working-class lives or cry out for social betterment, but in the sense that they comment, seriously, on the society we live in. Until enough time has passed to set our era in perspective, any such judgment as "*Look Back in Anger* is better than *Serjeant Musgrave's Dance*" (or *Roots* than *The Birthday Party*), is probably a matter of personal preference. What can be said is that all these plays are worthy of serious consideration.

There will probably always be what is so aptly called in France "un théâtre maudit"—a theatre which is damned; a theatre where, if produced at all, plays are supported only by a tiny minority of adventurous minds. This condemnation may arise from obtuseness, or from prudery, or simply from expediency. Critical obtuseness is too common to require comment; both Shaw and Ibsen ran up against the prudish spirit when they dared to tackle prostitution and venereal disease in *Mrs. Warren's Profession* and *Ghosts*; while expediency is responsible for all the plays which are never seen on the stage, and for those which are never written because the pressure against their inception is too great. Aristophanes, it should be remembered, wrote his great denunciation of war while the Peloponnesian War was actually in progress; an unimaginable theatrical venture for World War Two, when horror of war was inexpedient. So much is not expedient. Attack on Government policy. Attack on the Monarchy. Attack on the Church (not *very*).

Times change, of course, and we laugh at the prim horror revealed by the early Ibsen audiences. We grow more open-minded. We shift our ground about what is expedient, usually as a result of persistent hammering by individuals. But one factor remains constant: people do not like to be disturbed, to be forced to revalue their lives and way of thinking. There are certain subjects—the malaise of the time, if you like—of which people are aware, but which they do not wish to have brought out into the open and squarely faced. Take America, for instance, with the negro [sic] on her conscience. With all the mass of cinematic and theatrical material dealing with the negro problem, we have had to wait until the last two years (*A Man is Ten Feet Tall* and *Raisin in the Sun*) for the malaise to be conquered. The old magnanimous condescension has been jettisoned, to be replaced by an acceptance of the simple and obvious fact that, colour of skin apart, white and black are identical members of the human race, sharing the same preoccupations, the same aspirations. The problem remains, but the basic premises have shifted.

All things considered, Shaw and Ibsen, with their attacks on the late nineteenth century malaise of sex, were received into favour fairly rapidly. Well-bred audiences got used to the idea that you could hear prostitution and V.D. mentioned without peeping at your neighbour and reaching for the smelling-salts. But there is a long way from tolerating such references to accepting the implications. Ibsen and Shaw soon became cultural classics. Strindberg, however, had to fight harder for acceptance, and has never achieved the same popular consecration. Ibsen and Shaw treated sex and its appurtenances as a social fact: people *do* contract V.D.; prostitutes *do* exist; women *do* chafe at the chains of natural functions which bind them. These are facts which, ultimately, could not be denied. To Strindberg, sex, gathering strength from a long era of repression, was a motive force, something which governed behaviour and was all-pervasive. It was an imaginative conception, rather than a marshalling of truths. The result is that Strindberg's plays—*The Father, Dance of Death, Creditors, The Stronger,* for example—retain their theatrical power and excitement, while plays like *The Doll's House. Mrs. Warren's Profession* and *Misalliance* have dated, though spasmodically interesting. It was (and is) much easier to admit the validity of the arguments of Shaw and Ibsen than to recognise the truth of Strindberg. Man is, after all, a rational being, so we are told. The refusal to recognise Strindberg was not a refusal to admit the existence of certain sordid facts of life, but a refusal to accept that one was oneself involved in the sordidness.

The difference between the theatre of Shaw and Ibsen on the one hand, and Strindberg on the other, is one of approach. The civilised and the uncivilised. Social criticism or attack is acceptable, even when it kicks you in the belly, so long as you are looking. But Strindberg kicks you in the belly from behind. Which is unfair.

Saint's Day, The Birthday Party and *Serjeant Musgrave's Dance* share a common theme: the nature of violence. We are, as any reader of the daily press will know, living in an Age of Violence. The cinema, as any observer of C. A. Lejeune's weekly coy burial of her head in the sand will have noted, has placed its fingers squarely on this fact: brutality is served in liberal doses, usually for its own sake as a source of entertainment of growing popularity. Many films, however, have made a serious attempt to analyse violence in various contexts, not as something to relish and smack greedy chops over, but as something which is an integral part of our world and shapes our attitudes—notably, the films of Bunuel and Wajda. As far as the theatre is concerned (setting aside Genêt as too misrepresented in this country to have truly impinged), one can seize on moments only. The first act curtain of Donald Ogden Stewart's *The Kidders,* when the hero, left alone in his drawing-room cleaning an automatic-rifle (relic of army days), suddenly fires a random burst. "Just kidding, Baby," he explains to his frightened wife. Or, more acutely observed, the atmosphere of pending explosion in the first half of Ann Jellicoe's *Sport of My Mad Mother*; the ritual circling of the American stranger, caught in a blind-alley, by a group of Teddies; the terror of one of them who thinks he has killed the stranger, a terror slowly transmuted into exultation—"A treat . . . a fair treat . . . I feel good . . . I feel bloody good . . . I feel bloody wonderful." What Pinter, Arden and Whiting have done is to extend the responsibility for violence beyond the customary "What can you expect of Teddy-Boys?" (thugs/Reds/what-you-will) to "What can you expect of society?" The individual, unable to come to terms with society, unable or unwilling to place his ideals at its service, is crushed by society. And society, drained of its life-blood, slowly dies . . .

"There aren't any good, brave causes left," cried Jimmy Porter. This, precisely, is the inner dilemma of a world waiting today for the big bang, in an atmosphere of moral and social disintegration. The chain reaction of release is one of violence.

In *Saint's Day,* an elderly poet, Paul Southman, lives in a small village with his grand-daughter, Stella, and her husband. Twenty-five years ago he had written a bitter satirical pamphlet which went "straight into my Lady Society's chamber and lifted the skirts of the old whore." As a result, Society has ostracised him. Exiled, Southman has directed his satire against the villagers, so that something like a state of siege exists between the village and Southman's home. As the play opens, Southman is to be reinstated by Society at a dinner given in his honour: the emissary is "The Honourable Robert Procathren, distinguished young poet and critic, photographed last week after his marriage . . ." The old man, both frightened by, and hostile to, all that Procathren stands for, is suspicious. Stella's husband is a young painter who, hailed as a prodigy at fifteen, has since refused to show his paintings, afraid to open his inner self to a hostile world. Into this situation is thrown the news that the village is being terrorised by three soldiers who have escaped from a detention camp. The vicar of the village begs Southman for his aid against the marauders. Southman refuses, saying that he will join with the soldiers, to take his revenge on the village and on society. He taunts Procathren with his weakness and his intellectual theorising, and tricks him into taking a gun and joining them. The direct result is that Procathren accidentally kills Stella; accepting, for the first time, responsibility for his actions, he joins the marauders—he has been pushed too far. In the third act, it is he who leads the soldiers, he who precipitates the final holocaust in which the village is burnt, the villagers become refugees, and both Southman and the painter are hanged at Procathren's instigation.

The image is clear. It is an image of the disintegration of society, resulting in chaos. Southman is the visionary cast out by a society which had no need of him; now Stella suggests he may be needed—"Perhaps they have asked you to return because they need you. Perhaps they are in trouble out there and want your wisdom, your advice." Rejected by society, Southman now rejects society—"Why should I give them my advice? They are nothing to me." He refuses to listen to the vicar, who asks in all humility for his aid. He refuses Procathren who, in spite of his glossy-magazine overtones, genuinely sympathises with the older man's prophetic views. The real battle is between the creative mind (Southman) and Society in two guises (Procathren, the upper-class/intellectual, and the vicar, speaking for the lower-class/uneducated). The soldiers are merely the agents of destruction, waiting willingly to carry out any order from anybody who can, and will, give that order.

The Birthday Party, seven years later, follows a remarkably similar general plan, though the shifting social distinctions which this country has undergone are reflected in the play. The background—a seedy boarding-house in a seaside town—is even more precise than that of *Saint's Day,* but the agents of destruction have become anonymous, and are now in complete control. The disintegration has gone one stage further. In *Saint's Day,* Procathren takes command of the soldiers, as Southman might have done (and called them to heel), but in *The Birthday Party,* Goldberg and McCann give their own orders. Stanley, self-styled a concert pianist, has buried himself in the boarding-house. He never goes out, does not wash, does not work, is anti-social. The reason he gives for his self-burial is that, after one great concert success, "they" pulled a fast one; when he went down for his second concert, the hall was locked, and no one turned up. Whether Stanley is, or is not, an artist is left in doubt; the evidence (unlike the evidence for Southman) is deliberately contradictory. More direct is the evidence for Stanley's relationship with the elderly Meg, who runs the boarding-house, and Petey, her husband. Both regard him with genuine affection. Typical of Pinter's style is the deliberately ambiguous shifting of ground. In the opening scene, trying to get Stanley out of bed, Meg calls, "Stan! I'm coming up to fetch you if you don't come down! I'm coming up! I'm going to count three! One! Two! Three! I'm coming to get you!" Then, "So he's come down at last, has he? He's come down for his breakfast. But he dosen't deserve any, does he, Petey?" A few minutes later she enters into a grotesque and hilarious seduction scene with him. The mother-son, man-woman relationships are rapidly sketched in one movement by this ambiguity. Stanley, however, does not respond; he is consistently rude, and has one terrifyingly cruel scene in which he brainwashes Meg into believing that "they" have come to cart her away in a wheelbarrow (a reflection, incidentally, of his own fear). Petey's attitude to Stanley is calmer, almost imperceptible, until the final scene when he is "taken away" by Goldberg and McCann, and it is Petey who makes the protest; first, to Goldberg—"We can look after him here"—and then to Stanley himself—"Stan, don't let them tell you what to do!"

Unannounced, and apparently from nowhere, Goldberg and McCann arrive. A Jew and an Irishman, their speeches are full of oblique, shifting references to establishments against which the human being can sin: big business, the church, the I.R.A., test cricket, morality, and so on. It is Stanley's birthday (It it? Meg says so. Stanley denies it) and the visitors throw a nightmare party during which Stanley is hounded down, brainwashed, deprived of speech. In the morning he is carted off, clean, shaved, bowler-hatted and anonymous, to an unspecified fate. The image, again, is clear. Stanley has rejected society, both in the shape of his career and in the persons of Meg and Petey. Society, in the shape of Goldberg and McCann, takes its revenge.

In *Serjeant Musgrave's Dance,* four soldiers have deserted from their colonial regiment. They make their way, in mid-winter, to a Northern English town in the grip of a strike. Sick of the endless round of killing in which, as soldiers, they have been forced to participate, they plan to canvass recruits for their campaign against war and oppression. The coal-owner and local clergyman try to manipulate them as strike-breakers, "suggesting" possible recruits who would be useful out of the way. They agree to hold a recruiting rally. At the rally, they hoist the skeleton of a former comrade (a native of the town; this is bringing home the facts, with a vengeance). Holding the townspeople at gun-point, they hammer home their story of war. Internal dissensions make the plan break down, and it ends in fiasco with their arrest. The reason for the breakdown lies in the characters of the four soldiers. The leader, Serjeant Musgrave, stands revealed as a religious maniac who believes that he has been divinely appointed by God to administer a logical object lesson which will end all war; on the principle of an eye for an eye, he is to wreak retribution on those "responsible"—here, the coal-owner and the clergyman. The other three soldiers give him their allegiance for varying reasons. Sparky follows him blindly and in fear, even referring to him as "God," and constantly trying to escape his domination. The night before the rally, he tries to run away with the whore-barmaid, each of them hoping to find some sort of peace in the contact with another human being. He is killed by his comrades, Attercliffe and Hurst, when they try to prevent his escape. At the rally, after Musgrave's plea, the crowd still hesitates. Hurst, closest to Musgrave in outlook, but believing in human revenge rather than divine logic, urges that they open fire on the crowd. Musgrave protests. But it is the weaker-willed Attercliffe, sick with Sparky's blood on his hands, throws himself on Hurst's gun, with his mouth to the muzzle, to stop him from firing. At once, the crowd is lost. Someone asks where the fourth soldier is. Musgrave explains that he has been killed in an accident, that it makes no difference. "It makes all the difference" cries the barmaid. Again, the image is of destruction. Violence breeds violence. The soldiers are right in their denunciation, and the townspeople are right in their denunciation of the soldiers. But—when "bellies are full," when the town is free of strikes, oppression and hunger, when the atmosphere of violence is dispersed—*then* the message which the soldiers have brought will be remembered.

Each of these plays, over and above the common theme of violence, shares the fact that it creates its own distinctive world, with a mood and logic of urgency, directness and excitement, which makes nonsense of the critical reproach of obscurity and/or dullness. *Saint's Day*'s large, decaying manor, set in an atmosphere of hatred, where a trip to the village becomes a sortie into enemy territory, where the apocalyptic arrival of the marauding soldiers is terrifyingly announced by a Jericho trumpet, and where a crowd of frightened refugees passively watches the final holocaust. *The Birthday Party,* with its nightmare "no-exit" party, in which a game of blind-man's-buff is transformed into a maniacal witch-hunt, with an attempted murder punctuated in the darkness by the staccato beating of a toy drum. The cold, loveless, frozen wilderness of *Serjeant Musgrave's Dance,* where people live in silent fear and hatred, and where the frightened barmaid can find logical release in sleeping with a different man each night, seeking for contact; where the failure of the soldiers' plan is transformed into a macabre dance of death, with the townsfolk dancing, exulting, round the arrested soldiers.

Each of these plays creates a world before you, the audience, which you must enter, and whose rules you must inevitably follow. With each of them, if you do enter, you are swept along; their truths are hammered home, and you must accept, recognise, revalue. If you withhold your participation, you sit back in disbelief; these worlds become dull, obscure, meaningless.

A play like *Look Back in Anger* creates a world which, in essence, is familiar to us (reality, rather than an imaginative *dislocation* of reality), and it becomes easier for the mind to sidetrack onto an element which may be more pleasing to it than the main theme of the play. Constant reference is made, even by people who liked the play, to Jimmy Porter's *self-pity,* his *neurotic* behaviour, his *cruelty* to his wife. This makes nonsense of the play; Jimmy Porter is devoid of any neurosis or self-pity, and the play is summed up in his cry against a negative world, "Oh heavens, how I long for a little ordinary human enthusiasm. Just enthusiasm—that's all. I want to hear a warm, thrilling voice cry out Hallelujah! Hallelujah! I'm alive." (How Jimmy would have responded to Beatie Bryant in the closing moments of *Roots* . . .) Would *Look Back in Anger* have been the success it was if people had been forced to listen to this damning indictment of themselves as dead souls, instead of being allowed to stray into less dangerous channels (guying of English Sundays, excitingly turbulent sex-life, downtrodden and maltreated wife, etc.)? The same thing, I suspect, may be said of *Roots.*[1] In his preface to the published edition of the play, Arnold Wesker writes in a note, "My people are not caricatures . . . And though the picture I have drawn of them is a harsh one, yet still my tone is not of disgust." Obviously, in writing this note, Wesker felt that his Norfolk labourers might appear to be cruelly or maliciously presented. In fact, the portraits are warm, gentle and moving. In spite of the clarity and force with which Wesker develops his theme, it becomes easy enough to make the wrong response—"Well, they're really alright, fine people, no need to change anything." One can forget that Jimmy Beales, for example, harmlessly happy with his Territorial Jubilee to "Demonstrate and parade wi' arms and such like," driven to angry inarticulacy at Beatie's suggestion that the Hydrogen Bomb makes territorial arms look rather silly, is just the sort of man who answers the first call to serve King and Country without *ever* asking why.

A play which creates its own world, with its own relentless logic, forestalls any such wandering by the audience. Perhaps the price to be paid for such relentlessness is failure, commercial failure at least. A price which *Saint's Day, The Birthday Party* and *Serjeant Musgrave's Dance* have already paid.

[1] These remarks should not be construed in any way as derogatory to *Roots* or *Look Back in Anger*: simply as a comment on the reception of these fine plays.

Look Back in Anger

by A. E. Dyson

Look Back in Anger was first performed in Britain at the Royal Court Theatre on 8th May, 1956, and immediately became the outstanding dramatic success of a decade. It has suffered in critical discussion (though not in the box-office, so there are compensations) from the myth which almost immediately started to grow around it. The chief offenders have been what Jimmy Porter calls the 'posh papers', which seized on the play as a peg for yet more of the pseudo-sociology that has characterised the period (one wonders, retrospectively, how chimeras like 'outsiders', 'lucky Jims', 'angry young men' could have attracted so much attention whilst Rome was burning), and found in its hero a symbol of his whole generation, or at the very least of a 'movement' of some kind inside it. The phrase 'angry young men' was coined with direct reference to this play, and has since had a truly remarkable success. A year ago when the craze was still at its height, the term might have meant almost anything from a teddy-boy to a young don, or from a teen-aged pop-singer having his fifth breakdown to Lord Altrincham.

The myth is one thing that has distracted attention from the play. Another, possibly related, is the habit into which even serious critics have sometimes fallen of identifying Jimmy Porter with John Osborne, and treating the play as simple propaganda for its hero. The crudest form of this error is that which sees Jimmy as the spokesman of a movement, and his anger as pointing to some protest, or programme, or ideal which can be taken as the meaning of the play. The hero is regarded as straightforwardly admirable, and

"Look Back in Anger" by A. E. Dyson. From *The Critical Quarterly,* I, No. 4 (1959), 318-26.

his 'anger' as a finely directed critique of British society in the mid '50s. To my mind, such a reading is inadmissible for several important reasons. First, one has to say that no major drama is ever simple in this particular way. The moral impact of any except the crudest plays arises from the situation as a whole, not from uncritical committal to any one character in it. More specifically, in *Look Back in Anger* it is clear that certain enigmas touching both the hero himself, and the validity of his 'anger', are central to the effect. Jimmy Porter is not only a warm-hearted idealist raging against the evils of man and the universe, he is also a cruel and even morbid misfit in a group of reasonably normal and well-disposed people. This paradox in his status is inescapable, and the serious concern with the nature of evil, and of anger, which makes the play absorbing depends upon our continuing awareness of it. During the action, we witness a number of characters acting, interacting, discussing one another critically, making and retracting choices—and this in the setting of certain important symbols (the bears and squirrels, the church bells, the ironing-board, the trumpet and so on) which impose dramatic coherence, though not moral finality, on what happens. The construction is taut, and theatrically exciting; the ideas are stimulating, and the final effect is not of any kind of certainty —there is not even the degree of certainty offered by dramatic forms as definite as tragedy or comedy—but of realistic and challenging, enigma. As for Jimmy himself, one cannot doubt that a character so complex and troubled should owe something to his creator, any more than one would doubt that Shakespeare found the possibilities of Hamlet in himself, and Ibsen of Halvard Solness. But as with these other instances, it is impossible to imagine that the creator is identified with his creation, or even committed to approval untinged by irony and doubt. Such characters are placed in dramatic situations in which their potentialities for noble insight and creativity are balanced, and often overwhelmed, by inter-related capacities for ignoble and destructive illusions: the dramatic context, no less than the central character, embodies the intention of the writer. (*Hamlet,* if one likes to put it in this way, could not possibly have been written by Hamlet.)

In *Look Back in Anger,* the setting and action reflect searching irony on the hero, of a kind which forces us to see that even if John

Osborne intended elements of self-portrait, then he did so in no uncritical mood (the comparison with Gregers Werle, Ibsen's savagely ironic self-portrait in *The Wild Duck,* might strike us as parallel). Again: if Jimmy is offered as a 'typical' hero, he is so as Hamlet is—a recognisable and recurring type, perhaps, also, a permanent possibility in the make-up of any sensitive person; but in a minority in any generation, and in most individuals resolutely suppressed.

II

How, then, have the myth and the oversimplified interpretation grown up? Partly through the author's undoubted concern for the contemporary scene, which is no less striking when one ceases to think of Jimmy Porter as a 'typical' hero. And then, because of the sheer authenticity of the play's background, a factor which adds the pleasures of recognition to other pleasures for a contemporary audience, and perhaps draws attention too exclusively to the sociological implications. 'Authenticity' I have called it, and I think this is justified, despite the fact that some of the details (Jimmy's supposed university background, for instance, and the notion that he would in all seriousness be running a sweet-stall endowed by a well-disposed charwoman) are far from convincing in themselves. Such details disturb slightly, but in its larger impact the play rings unerringly true. Take, for instance, the peculiar *quality* of frustration in Jimmy's anger—a quality which seems to make such solutions as committal to a party or a cause hopelessly inaccessible to him. Though the hydrogen bomb is mentioned only twice, one feels throughout its pervasive effect upon the moral imagination of a generation: the limits which it sets, both to personal heroism, and to the future, as incentives to hope and action. Remembering the type of participation in Spain which seemed possible to intellectuals of Jimmy's type in 1937, and the inevitable paralysis imposed on their counterparts at the time of Hungary twenty years later, one can feel that this play is aware of the psychological impact of the H-Bomb era upon men like Jimmy as subtly as anything else in recent literature. Again, consider the place of 'the establishment' in the play. Protests against insensitivity and hypocrisy in Church and

State have been more or less constant features of western civilisation, at least since those of Christ himself, and Jimmy's main complaints are little different in content from those of (say) D. H. Lawrence thirty years before. But the tone is different, and distinctive. It belongs to a generation which comes after the second world war, after the Attlee administration, and is becoming aware in this new situation of the perennial success of conventional morality in its war against those who try to take its own ideals too seriously. One's final feeling is that one is hearing the age-old voice of moral outrage, but hearing it authentically in our own time and setting.

There is authenticity, too, in the manner in which Cliff's casually comfortable place in the household is accepted, and in Jimmy's feeling that sexual fidelity is infinitely less important to him than the moral and spiritual fidelity which he fails to find in Alison. In earlier periods, even in our own century, the basic situation would very probably have been the occasion either for a justification of 'unconventional' against 'conventional' sexual *mores,* or for some psychological probing in Freudian or other terms. In this play, Jimmy, Alison and Cliff (though not, of course, Helena), take their relationship in these respects for granted. In this they are, I think, typical; and here as elsewhere *Look Back in Anger* makes new advances in the depiction of social realism.

III

When this is allowed, one comes back to the character of Jimmy Porter himself (and I should confess here, no doubt, that I think a Bradleian approach to the play, in terms of character, is likely to be at least as illuminating as any other). What does one feel about Jimmy? Obviously, he is not ideal. He suffers, is frustrated, and makes terribly wrong choices (as the last scene makes clear, even for those who imagine that his blasphemy against life when he hopes that Alison 'will have a baby, and that it will die' is a mere expression of the playwright's sense of values). The case against him is not one that can be made with any suspicion that one is catching John Osborne out: clues of the most explicit kind are provided in the very first stage direction.

> . . . Jimmy is a tall, thin young man about twenty-five, wearing a very worn tweed jacket and flannels . . . He is a disconcerting mixture of sincerity and cheerful malice, of tenderness and free-booting cruelty; restless, importunate, full of pride, a combination which alienates the sensitive and insensitive alike. Blistering honesty, or apparent honesty, like his, makes few friends. To many he may seem sensitive to the point of vulgarity. To others, he is simply a loudmouth. To be as vehement as he is is to be almost non-committal.

The doubts suggested here by 'or apparent honesty', 'to the point of vulgarity', 'almost non-committal' are sufficiently striking: and from Jimmy's first appearance, his anger is no less ambiguous than himself. It is a commonplace of morality to point out that anger can be anything from an indispensable virtue to a most degrading and dangerous vice, and that between these extremes every shade of reality and illusion, nobility and viciousness, can often be detected. Notoriously, it is a chameleon emotion, changing colour and mood unnoticed, and subtly allowing the best in a man to offer sanctions to the worst. Between the righteous indignation of Christ upbraiding the Pharisees, or of Blake contemplating an Albion which burns little boys for their innocence, and the spoilt petulance of a child or a tyrant, there are great ranges in which anger can work, and numerous occasions for good men, whose anger starts in outraged justice, to become bad. A moralist might offer specific reflections on this, as, for example, that anger is good when it is selfless, compassionate and allied to positive action, evil when it is selfish, or tainted with bitterness, frustration and the desire to hurt. A creative artist dealing with the emotion is more likely to be alive to ways in which most anger hovers between these two poles in most actual men and situations; and Osborne's *Look Back in Anger* is a moral exploration in exactly this field. In Jimmy Porter, one is confronted with a man whose anger undoubtedly starts in human idealism, and the desire that men should be more honest, more alive, more human than they normally are. Very soon, however, corruption creeps in: his sense of outrage is so little controlled by either selflessness, stoicism or any clear discipline of the mind, that it readily degenerates into moods profoundly and dangerously maladjusted. The alarming juxtapositions in his make-up, with a holy crusade against stupidity on the one side, and a neurotic shrinking from in-laws and church bells on the other, cannot be escaped. His motives are hopelessly mixed: one can never be sure whether his anger with Alison starts in a genuine desire to save her, or in an ugly type of possessiveness heavily disguised. His targets are inconsistent: he lashes at Cliff both for not reading the *New Statesman* and for reading it; he taunts his wife with her education, and Cliff with his ignorance. From the start, it is clear that, rightly or wrongly, he has not acquired the normal techniques for accepting suffering, and that he regards his almost morbid sensitivity to it as evidence of moral superiority. He becomes convinced that he is the only one who really *knows* what suffering is, and that he has the right to scourge those less agitated than himself. There are marked symptoms of a persecution-complex, both in the tenacity with which he clings to his working class origin as an occasion for masochism, and in his readiness to see his wife's continued correspondence with her parents in terms of conspiracy and betrayal. His tenderness for his wife (the real tenderness implied in the bears and squirrels game as well as elsewhere) is unable to survive the restless suspicions which turn love into conquest, marriage into revenge, and the normal reticences of others into insult. More sinister than this, he has the iconoclasm peculiar to that most dangerous type, the frustrated Messiah, who because he cannot save the world comes to feel the desire to destroy it instead. Much of the time, his deeds and imagery are deliberately calculated to shock. In attempting to hurt his wife he outrages every decency of love and of life itself, the certainty of his moral mission to her merely justifying every savagery of tone and mood he can command. All of this goes, as one might expect, with a peculiar sensitivity to shock on his own part. He can accept neither life, nor death, with ease; the sound of church bells torments him with the thought of possible worlds other than his own.

Doubts about his sanity are inescapable; in this sense, he is remarkably like Hamlet, though in a smaller, and domestic, setting. Like Hamlet, he lacks the power to relate his powerful emotional revulsion against evil either to a rational appraisal of the universe as a whole or to adequate self-knowledge. His failure in this respect is certainly a moral flaw, and might even be a symptom of madness. Like Hamlet, he sees something rotten in the state, and the rottenness is not all of his own imagining. Yet his response, again like Hamlet's, is to lay about him on all sides—using words as a lash (some of his outbursts are reminiscent of the bedroom scene in Act IV of *Hamlet*), killing where he loves as well as where he hates, finding guilt in the blameless and the mediocre as well as in the really vile (though he does know that 'mummy' is worse than 'daddy', and his anger is not entirely undiscriminating): his insight mingled with illusion, his idealism with cruelty, his desire to save with an appalling capacity for destruction.

Jimmy Porter, however, if a Hamlet figure in some respects, has less basic nobility of mind, less talent, less sense of destiny than Hamlet; the setting is domestic, and his destructiveness only once approaches physical violence. Self-pity plays a larger role in his consciousness, readily assimilating his genuine insight to a certain smallness, as well as perversity, of mind. Though his impieties are often safely and admirably based, the pieties that should balance them—whether to God, or Man, or Nature as they *might* be beyond the mazes of human error—are nowhere clearly realised. In this, he differs disastrously from any hero that Blake or Lawrence, agreeing with his negative criticisms, might have offered. His genuine affection for Cliff, and love for Alison, are at the mercy of his anger rather than directing it as they should. His trumpet can mock the universe, but not sound a call to battle; he becomes an emotional liability to those he seeks to inspire.

In all this, Osborne's main concern, like that of Shakespeare on his much larger canvas, seems to be to tell the truth of a situation, not to offer final moral reflections on it. As I suggested earlier, those who imagine that the doubts about Jimmy's character which have been concerning us here somehow escaped the attention of his creator must have a strangely naive notion of how plays come to be written. On the other hand, those who imagine that the case against Jimmy is all that the play offers overlook certain other data which are at least equal in their importance. First, both Alison and Cliff, and later even Helena, feel that Jimmy is a basically worthwhile character. They may not be convinced by his ideas, and Alison at one stage decides that her sanity depends upon getting away from him, but they never doubt that his torment is at root that of a good man, not of a bad one, and that he deserves success, even if he seems unlikely to find it. Also, they sense that his anger has in it elements of honesty and courage that might be redemptive if it could ever be released into effective action. (Helena thinks that he is born out of his time, and should have lived in the French Revolution; Alison's image of him is always that of the knight in armor.) In matters of personal morality, he stands resolutely opposed to Pharisees and Laodiceans alike: he is on the side of engagement, whatever else can be said.

IV

Before summing up, it might be helpful to look briefly at his relationship with the two women in the play. First, because this is easier to deal with, with Helena. Helena is an entirely honest character from an entirely different world from Jimmy's. She is middle-class not only by birth but by instinct and conviction: this is why she is essentially disruptive to Jimmy, both when she conspires against him, and when she is his mistress. This, also, is why she can never really hurt him as Alison can. She interferes with his marriage for Alison's good, since she honestly thinks (and this need not even be a rationalisation) that Alison will be better out of the 'madhouse'; and she takes Jimmy for herself because she finds that she loves him, and wants to have him. At no stage, however, does she allow her values to be questioned by Jimmy's, so that he can never think that she has come over into his camp, or be hurt by any sense of betrayal. She believes all along that her love is sinful, 'terribly wrong', as she tells Alison, and she knows in the end that Alison has 'all the rights', and will have to come back. Whereas Jimmy lives at war with the conventions, and believes that sincerity alone can govern human relationships, Helena is equally sure that the 'book of rules' is necessary to sanity, and says

> At least, I still believe in right and wrong! Not even the months in this madhouse have stopped me doing that. Even though everything I have done is wrong, at least I have known it was wrong.

The affair between them has never touched her at the deepest level, and the fact that her loyalty to conventions—whether through conviction, or fear, or even thoughtlessness scarcely matters—comes even before her loyalty to people makes this partly inevitable. Jimmy knows, presumably, that in this they are opposites, so that when she leaves him, making the break with a toughness characteristic of her kind, he is resigned rather than angry, and hurt only at the level of personal response, not at the level of his ideals.

Alison is far nearer to Jimmy, since he is trying to win not only her love, but her allegiance to his own vision of life—a vision in which the 'book of rules' must be shut at the start, and true committal worked out in individual terms. He comes to feel, as we have seen, that Alison has betrayed him, by seeming to come over to him in marriage whilst remaining mentally and spiritually in the world of her parents. In a sense he is right, as her habits of thought when she leaves him, and even more when she discusses him with her father, make clear. She has responded to physical love, but not offered it; listened to ideas, but withheld enthusiasm; submitted to the attraction of Jimmy as a knight, but clung obstinately to the security of well-bred indifference in the face of his onslaughts. The most telling criticism of her attitude is made (interestingly) by her father, who says that like himself she enjoys sitting on the fence. She is surprised, and even hurt by this: 'I married him, didn't I?' is her immediate reply. But this middle-class defence clearly does not convince even her father, who sees as clearly as Jimmy himself that she has never given herself to her husband with the honesty that she knows he demands and needs.

The ending of the play in this respect is ambiguous. Jimmy, confronted with her real suffering and degradation, and the appalling knowledge that this is what, in his anger, he has been demanding of her, himself breaks under the strain and has to appeal for mercy. The confrontation seems to awaken him to the blasphemy, and immaturity, of his excesses of anger, and possibly purges it in that moment. Alison herself, having really suffered, and then come back, can be presumed to have realised her own defects, and to have returned with the intention of a deeper committal to Jimmy's values. They revert to the bears and squirrels game, as a refuge from a world which sets 'cruel steel traps' for its animals. It seems likely (to the present writer, at least), that this basis of warm, animal love might, on the other side of real suffering and committal, lead to a happy, and continuing relationship. Some critics feel otherwise, however, and see in the ending merely a temporary escape from realities, probably tragic, which will have to be faced later. Both possibilities are left open, and remarkably so in a play which is often said to be propagandist in aim.

V

The reconciliation between Jimmy and Alison, though important, is not the final resolution of the play, which also challenges us with unresolved problems concerning the reconciliation between Jimmy and the universe. What do we make of this?

First, I think the play's impact lies in making its audience realise that questions they might have considered closed are really open, and that attitudes they might have taken for granted are really controversial. It is a challenging play in the last instance, and challenging not brashly, as Jimmy's anger is, but with the thoughtfulness behind the playwright's manipulation of the situation as a whole.

In one sense, the challenges are fairly simple, and might be put crudely. Do we really think (and this is Jimmy's own challenge) that the voice raised in protest must always be a weakling's voice? Might it not, sometimes, be raised in strength, and with authority? Is failure to be at home in a society in which we have 'never had it so good' simply adolescent maladjustment, or might it not be at least the beginning of grace? Is our awareness of sickness in Jimmy's anger all that needs to be said about it, or is the major sickness in society itself, which reduces potential knights to raging impotence? Osborne's honesty in exploring the ambiguities and weaknesses of anger is such that he allows escape, by way of such familiar routes as 'What are the angry young men really angry about?', 'Can't they take it like men?' to those who prefer the status-quo. But this escape is itself a form of trap, in that those who unreflectingly take it proclaim themselves moral cripples on the other side. To admire Jimmy Porter uncritically is to distort. Anyone with the least concern for human values, however, is bound to find in his anger not only evidences of immaturity, but also the type of conscience, and engagement, without which any supposed moral maturity can be no more than a sham.

Look Back in Anger is a play which increases understanding both of the tormented and their torments. But it does more. It reminds us what our rebel moralists are apt to be like, and of the strange mingling of sensitivity and cruelty, insight and wilfulness, idealism and cynicism in their make-up that can make life terrible for those who know them, and yet offer rewards as well.

In a world which usually deals with its most challenging moral misfits by first mocking or martyring them, and later venerating them for the wrong reasons, it is no bad thing for writers to remind us occasionally what such people are often really like.

Godot and His Children: The Theatre of Samuel Beckett and Harold Pinter

by Martin Esslin

January 5, 1953, the day when Samuel Beckett's play *Waiting for Godot* opened its stage career at the tiny (and since defunct) Théâtre de Babylone on the Paris Left Bank, may well become a milestone in the history of drama. For, although other authors had preceded Beckett with plays in a similar vein (Ionesco with *The Bald Prima Donna* and Arthur Adamov with *L'Invasion,* both first staged in 1950, and Jean Tardieu with *Qui est là* as early as 1949), the eventual triumph of *Waiting for Godot* constituted the breakthrough into the public consciousness of a new convention of drama which, for want of a better, has been vaguely labelled with the tentative generic term of the 'Theatre of the Absurd'. *Waiting for Godot,* written and originally performed in French, has since been translated into some twenty languages and, having been performed from Finland to the Argentine, from Ireland to Japan, has become a contemporary classic—and all that within ten years of its first performance.

The most astonishing fact about the success of this play—and others in the same convention of writing—is undoubtedly the circumstance that by all established canons of drama it is not a play at all and should therefore not be capable of achieving any effect on an audience: for if a good play, according to all the accepted canons of drama, must have a beginning in which the characters are presented and the plot given its exposition, a middle in which the plot is ravelled up, and an end in which it is neatly unravelled, this play has no exposition, no middle, and no end: the final situation is exactly the same as the opening one and the characters have been neither presented nor explained when the final curtain falls. If the good play in the established taste has to give deep psychological insights into the thought and feelings of the characters, this, if anything, obscures them; if the well-made play is required to excel in witty dialogue and brilliant repartee, this play is distinguished by dialogue which is constantly exposed as an abortive attempt at communication; and if the glory of the well-made play is the truth and consistency of character drawing, here the characters are not even, from one scene to the next, sure that they are talking to the same people. And yet, this strange play, condemned to failure by all established touchstones of critical judgment, has, as an empirical fact, amused, intrigued, annoyed, but also immensely moved large audiences, not only on the stage, but also on television and radio.

What, then, if it lacks all the criteria of established dramatic excellence, does *Waiting for Godot,* give its audience?

The play is in two acts, each of which follows almost exactly the same pattern. On an empty stage representing a country road, bare but for a single sickly tree, two men, dressed in tattered clothes and ancient bowler hats are trying to keep an appointment. They are not too sure whether they really have this appointment, nor whether this is the place or the time that had been agreed. Nor are they too sure with whom the appointment is to be and what its purpose is. The two men, Vladimir and Estragon (but we are never quite sure that these are their names: Vladimir is at times called Mr. Albert and Estragon, when asked, says his name is Catullus) are in some ways complementary natures: Estragon is emotional and a poet, Vladimir more rational and down-to-earth. They are dependent on each other and yet want to get away from each other; and above all they are convinced of the desirability of doing away with themselves. But each time they attempt to commit suicide, they fail through sheer incompetence. In each of the two acts Vladimir and Estragon meet another pair of characters: Pozzo and Lucky. Pozzo is big, fat, and opulent; Lucky thin, bedraggled, and old, is

Pozzo's slave, driven by him with a whip and with a halter round his neck; the only development is that in the second act Pozzo is stricken with blindness and now Lucky's halter serves as the blind man's lead. . . . The two pairs of characters meet in each act, try to communicate, fail and part: Vladimir and Estragon remain waiting, Pozzo and Lucky resume their wanderings. At the end of each act a little boy appears; he brings a message from Godot: Godot cannot come today, but he will come without fail—tomorrow. . . .

And what do Estragon and Vladimir, Pozzo and Lucky have to say to each other? While they wait, Estragon and Vladimir try to pass the time by starting some sort of conversation: various topics recur in a seemingly haphazard fashion: the two thieves on the crosses next to that of the Saviour and why one of them was saved and one was damned, the leaves falling and the transitoriness of life in time; suicide; the mysterious way in which Estragon's shoes sometimes fit him and sometimes are far too tight. . . . Pozzo boasts. Lucky who, as Pozzo says, taught him all he knows, is silent except for a performance he gives at his master's bidding. He is told to 'think' and produces an endless and almost wholly nonsensical speech which parodies scientific and philosophical argument. In the second act, when Pozzo has gone blind, Lucky has been struck dumb.

What are we to make of it all? I think that already from my attempt to give an account of the contents of the play certain conclusions emerge. In the case of most other plays one would convey their quality by telling their *story.* In this case I had started off by telling you something about the *pattern,* the repetitive construction of the play. Moreover, I was unable to say anything definite about the characters or the situation. In fact I ended up by leaving both characters and situation open, by asking *questions* about them rather than making *statements.* So that we can say that in *Waiting for Godot* the narrative, story-telling, plot-making element of drama is missing and so is the touch of certainty with which a dramatic author usually presents his characters. If we follow a play by Ibsen—or Rattigan—attentively we should *know* what kind of people we are confronted with. Here we are made to *wonder* whether they are people at all or merely fleeting apparitions of an author's wayward imagination. If in the well-made play the core of the drama is *action, happenings,* here the very purpose of the play is to say that *nothing happens*—nothing really happens in human life. *Waiting for Godot* is thus a living paradox: a drama—and drama means action—of inaction.

A pattern of uncertainties and questions, an action demonstrating the absence of action—here we have the essence of Beckett's play. And if we look at it a little more closely—and without any of the preconceived notions of what drama ought to be, we can see quite clearly what Beckett wants to express: human beings waiting for the arrival of someone or something with whom they may or may not have an appointment. Are we not all born into this world without knowing what our purpose is, are we not all, now that we are here, assuming that perhaps we have a purpose and that the next day will bring the moment of revelation—and then night falls and we are told to try again tomorrow and so on for ever after? Are we not all, whether we just hang around waiting like the two tramps, or rush madly about like Pozzo, trying to give our life some purpose, trying to while away the time in some fashion, knowing full well that without that final knowledge about what we are here for, all our activities are merely futile antics? And are we not all, like Pozzo and Lucky, subject to the most sudden reversals of our fortunes, hale and hearty one day, blind and helpless the next? Are not all our most clever attempts at thinking and theorising, like Lucky's, ultimately reducible to an empty rush of meaningless words, and shall we not all in the end, like Lucky, be struck dumb? And are we not all, as social beings, irrevocably tied to each other, however much we might loathe each other's company, simply because one human being can never live in isolation and yet all contact between human beings inevitably produces friction—as between Vladimir and Estragon—or dominance and subjection—as between Pozzo and Lucky?

These are only a few of the themes of *Waiting for Godot* which I am trying to pick out from the intricate pattern of images of the human condition which Beckett has here intertwined with great art and complexity in the same way in which the musical themes of a symphony are interwoven in an infinitely complex pattern of statement and counter-statement, consonance and contrast. Complex patterns of this kind are the hallmark of music and poetry. And here we have, in my opinion, the clue to the understanding of *Waiting for Godot* and of the other plays in this convention: these plays are not like the conventional well-made drama re-enacted *stories,* they are complex and extended *poetic images* brought to life before the eyes of the audience. If the drama of plot and character is akin to the *narrative* art, this type of play is essentially *lyrical.* If the conventional, well-made play unrolls before our eyes like a comic strip in which the action proceeds from point A to point B, in this type of drama, as in a poem, we are witnessing the unfolding of a static pattern as that of a flower which gradually opens and reveals a structure that, however, has been present from the beginning. The two types of drama consequently have a completely different kind of suspense. In the conventional play we ask: what is going to happen next? How is it going to end? In this kind of play we ask: what is happening? What is the nature of the pattern that is unfolding?

It is from this really fundamental difference in aim between the two types of drama that we can deduce the nature of the effect of the new kind of play on its audience. For here the audience is presented not with a ready-made sequence of events with a manifest intention and meaning, here the audience is asked to contribute something of its own: it is up to each member of the audience to reach his own conclusion as to *what he is going to make of the play.* It is in the mind of the spectator that the multifarious strands of meaning will finally form into a more or less intricate pattern, according to how many of the numerous motifs and themes he has been able to respond to. This explains the exasperation produced on some, the deep cathartic effect evoked in others. It is highly irritating to be confronted with a pattern that one cannot see; it is, on the other hand, highly gratifying to perceive what, at first glance is a mysterious jumble which suddenly falls into place and becomes a meaningful pattern in front of one's eyes.

Nor does one have to be specially sophisticated to respond to an artistic experience of this kind. On the contrary. The more one approaches a novel convention with the expectations and the conditioning of an elaborate education as to what one is to look for in a work of art, the less will one be able to discern its aims and beauties. When *Waiting for Godot* was performed in front of the inmates of San Quentin Penitentiary in California (by the San Francisco Actors' Workshop who went there with considerable trepidation) the audience not only responded enthusiastically, they also immediately saw the point of the play: Godot for them was the hope of the miraculous release which they could never entirely discard from their thought; and to see that all human beings, in their own fashion, are confronted with a similar futility gave them some relief and consolation.

If the theatre of plot and character involves the audience emotionally by enabling them to identify themselves with the heroes of its plays and thus to experience their emotions and triumphs vicariously, this kind of theatre which confronts its audience with a concrete pattern of poetic images demands a positive effort of interpretation, and appeals at the same time to a very deep layer of the subconscious mind. In this the Theatre of the Absurd is analogous to abstract painting and sculpture which also grip the spectator both on the level of the archetypal image that strikes chords in the deepest layers of the mind and on the level of a highly intellectual interpretative effort. The same is true of our response to poetry: the rhythm and colour of a poem, its tonal and associative qualities appeal to the deepest strata of the mind, while it can also appeal to the intellect through the precision and elegance of its expression, the depths of the thought it propounds.

Samuel Beckett, an Anglo-Irishman born in Dublin in 1906, is an innovator and explorer who nevertheless forms part of a tradition: Swift, Kafka, Joyce, Proust, the Surrealists have formed his writing as much as the cross-talk of Irish music-hall comedians (strongly present in the dialogue of *Waiting for Godot*) and the knockabout comedy of the silent film (the two tramps wear Chaplin's battered bowler and gaping boots, their relationship recalls such pairs as Laurel and Hardy). Beckett's dramatic work cannot be fully understood without his narrative prose which, in my opinion, ranks him among the foremost writers of our age.

It is highly significant that Beckett's *œuvre* mirrors some of the fundamental preoccupations of contemporary philosophy. Although Beckett himself is not aware of any such influence, his writings might be described as a literary exposition of Sartre's Existentialism.

Existential philosophy starts from the rejection of the validity and reality of general concepts. In idealistic philosophy such concepts as 'goodness' or 'beauty' are regarded as real. Anything that is good and beautiful contains as it were a reflection, a particle of the 'good', the 'beautiful'; the particular mirrors, the eternal essences, the platonic ideas. Thus in idealistic philosophy *essence* comes before *existence*. But, so the existential philosopher argues, these platonic ideas, these eternal essences, are mere abstractions from the concrete, the particular. So the primary must always be the concrete, the existing, which is always something particular, individual, unique—and therefore, *existence comes before essence*. General truths, ethical systems, thus become mere illusions. Each individual has to work out his own salvation by himself, for, encapsuled in his own particularity, he is utterly alone. For him, and for him alone, the good, the true, and the beautiful derive entirely from his own experience. What is good or true for one, may bear no relation to what is good and true for another individual. The quality of the individual's experience becomes decisive. Each individual has his own *sense of being*. Beckett's work, both in his novels and in his plays, constitutes just such an exploration of being. What is the essence of the experience of being? asks Beckett. And so he begins to strip away the inessentials. What is the meaning of the phrase 'I am myself'? he asks . . . and is then compelled to try to distinguish between the merely accidental characteristics that make up an individual and the essence of his self.

To simplify the issue: let us assume that a girl loves a handsome, clever young man, X. What does she mean when she says she loves X? Are his good looks, for example part of his essential self? He might lose an arm in an accident. Would his girl still love him, then? Perhaps. But what if he lost both legs and both arms? Would X then still *be* X, and lovable as X's self as far as his girl is concerned? Perhaps. But then she might be in love not with his body but with his wit and his spiritual qualities. What, then, if X lost not only his limbs but also his mind—if he went mad? Would that half-witted trunk still *be* X, would it have any identity with the young, intelligent, athletic X? Would there still be anything to love in it for a girl who loved X in his previous shape? And yet in some sense there would be some identity between the two stages of X's development. The question merely is: in what sense?

It is to explore these very fundamental questions that Beckett again and again introduces such human flotsam into his works: the father and mother in the dustbins in *Endgame,* legless, senile, disgusting—and yet still musing on their honeymoon when they bicycled together on a tandem. Cyclists then—legless now; or Malone the dying paralysed wreck of a man in the novel, *Malone Dies;* or the nameless fragment of a man, already dead or as yet unborn, who is seeking for an identity in *The Unnamable;* or Krapp in the short play *Krapp's Last Tape,* an old, broken man who listens to the tape of his own voice from his own youth and cannot find himself in that utterly strange recording.

The search for man's own identity—not the *finding* of the true nature of the self which for Beckett will remain ever elusive, but the raising of the problem of identity itself, the confrontation of the audience with the existence of its own problematical and mysterious condition; this, fundamentally, is the theme of Beckett's plays, novels, prose sketches, and poems.

Such a quest, despairing and nihilistic as it may appear (for at the centre of being there is a void, nothingness) is nevertheless a very lofty enterprise—for it is totally fearless, dedicated and uncompromising; it is, in the last resort a religious quest in that it seeks to confront the ultimate reality. If it has more in common with Buddhism, Indian mysticism (or some forms of Christian mysticism as well) rather than with the commonly accepted forms of religious thought in the West, this does not alter its basically religious quality. To regard Beckett as a purveyor of sordidness, simply because he deals with human beings at the limits of their selfhood, to label him a 'dustbin dramatist' is therefore the height of insensitiveness and ignorance of his true aims.

Beckett's influence on contemporary literature is only beginning to make itself felt. But it is certainly a noteworthy fact that one of the most promising young playwrights in this country, Harold Pinter, acknowledges Beckett, together with Kafka, as the main influence on his work. This influence is a very deep one, in spite of the fact that a superficial observer might not notice it at all. For Harold Pinter's success with the public—and with most of the critics—is largely due to a factor which certainly does not derive from Beckett (who writes most of his serious work in French, a language which is not his mother-tongue and which therefore forces him into a highly stylised, classical mould). Harold Pinter (born in London in

1930) has a phenomenally sensitive ear for the real speech of real people. His dialogue is, superficially at least, of a devastating naturalness. He not only captures the vocabulary of real conversation but also the varied quirks of repetition, malapropism, tautology, spurious logic, and verbal incantation which pervade ordinary speech and which, hitherto, had been largely missed in stage dialogue that attempted to combine naturalness with good grammar, correct vocabulary and logical progression of its reasoning. Pinter's 'tape-recorder fidelity' has opened up a new dimension of stage dialogue; and as such it can be wildly funny.

This knack of naturalness has led some critics to class Pinter with the social realists among the new wave of British playwrights, the 'kitchen-sink school'. The affinity of his work with this group of playwrights, however, is a very superficial one. For Pinter is not a realist in their sense at all. He is not concerned with social questions, he fights for no political causes. Like Beckett he is essentially concerned with communicating a 'sense of being', with producing patterns of poetic imagery, not in words so much as in the concrete, three-dimensional happenings that take place on the stage. Like Beckett, Pinter wants to communicate the mystery, the problematical nature, of man's situation in the world. However natural his dialogue, however naturalistic some of his situations may superficially appear, Pinter's plays are also basically images, almost allegories, of the human condition.

This can be seen quite clearly in Pinter's first play, *The Room* (1957), which contains, as in embryo, much of the subject-matter of his later, more mature and accomplished efforts. He himself has told the story of the origin of this play. Looking at two people in a room, a room with a door, he was suddenly struck by the idea that the very existence of that door contained a menace. For at any moment the door might open—and who, or what, might enter? In other words, Pinter was suddenly struck with the precariousness of the situation in which we all find ourselves. All rooms have doors; wherever we are, we are separated from the unknown, the vast darkness of the universe and its mystery, from death, by the thinnest and flimsiest of partitions. Our own consciousness, our awareness of ourselves is a small pool of light surrounded by a vast outer darkness. It is this feeling which is dramatised in the play, *The Room*.

The ageing woman only knows her own room, she likes its warmth, its cosiness and is constantly terrified of losing it. The vast house in which the room is situated is a mystery to her, she does not even know how many floors it has, she only knows that the basement is dark and damp. And then the door does open, there are people outside, they have been told there is a room to let in the house, this very room. . . . This is a dramatic effect very characteristic of Pinter: terror achieved with the simplest and, on the surface, most natural means. At the end of the play the door opens again: this time a blind negro [sic] enters who is obviously an allegorical figure, a messenger of dark powers, of death. He is calling the woman 'home'. Pinter himself now criticises this element in his first play for the over-obviousness of its symbolic machinery. In his later work the allegorical, supernatural element recedes into the background. Stanley, the hero of *The Birthday Party,* for example, has also found a cosy home—in a sleezy seaside boarding-house where he is being mothered by the landlady. Here too the heralds of the outside world appear to drive Stanley from the warmth of his security. But these two men are very realistically drawn characters, an Irishman and a Jew. We never learn *why* they are after Stanley, merely that they have come to terrorise him and to take him away. They might be members of a political party or spy ring he has deserted, they might be sent by his family who want to bring him back to respectability or they may be messengers of death. Their nature is never explained. The play merely conveys the poetic image of the kind of nameless menace they represent.

Pinter's most successful play to date, *The Caretaker,* reverses the same situation: here we have a man *seeking* for a place for himself, fighting for that little patch of light and warmth in the vast menacing darkness. He has every chance of being given such a place by Aston and Mick, the two brothers who own the strange, derelict apartment where Aston lives. In fact Aston has brought Davies, the tramp, to his place after rescuing him from a scuffle in a café. But Davies is so selfish, so overconfident, that he cannot resist the temptation of playing off the two brothers against each other—and so, at the end of the play he is expelled again into the cold outer darkness. On one level *The Caretaker* is a realistic play, almost a slice of life, but on another, deeper level it is a poetic image of the human condition itself: Man fighting for a place, for security, but at the same time deprived of it by the weakness of his own fallible, selfish nature. Behind the drab happenings between a tramp and two ordinary men there thus stands the great primeval issue of original sin, man's expulsion from Paradise. . . .

Far from being a member of the kitchen-sink school, therefore, Harold Pinter is a maker of myths, a real poet, both in his subject matter and imagery, and in his use of language. For here too the naturalness of his dialogue is deceptive. It has the rhythm, the strangeness, and by its very repetitiveness, the incantatory quality of poetry.

Harold Pinter is still too young to allow us to give a definitive assessment of his stature or achievement. If he fulfils his promise (after all he only started to write plays in 1957 and has veritably rocketed to fame) he may well become one of the most important playwrights of our time. For already his achievement points the way towards the future: he has shown that it is possible to combine the poetic imagery, the 'open' construction of the Theatre of the Absurd with techniques which do not deviate too much from the mainstream of the tradition of drama. Pinter's plays do away with lengthy exposition, they leave the action and the characters unmotivated and unexplained, they reach no neat solution or conclusion, they raise questions rather than answer them, they force the audience to find their own interpretations, and yet, simultaneously, these plays are perfectly acceptable as representations of life, as observations of ordinary human behaviour.

But, you may ask, why should Beckett and Pinter—and the other dramatists of the Absurd: Ionesco, Adamov, N. F. Simpson, Edward Albee, Genet, Arrabal, and others—why should they have tried to destroy the well-made play, why should they have done away with exposition and motivations at the beginning, neat solutions of all the questions raised at the end of plays? Why should they have destroyed the unity of character, so that the tramps in *Waiting for Godot* are never certain whether the Pozzo they meet in the second act is the same person as the one they met in the first?

My answer to these questions is simply this: drama, the theatre, always reflects the cultural situation, the thought of its time. I have already shown how closely Beckett's plays are linked with existential philosophy. But the correspondences between contemporary thought and the avant-garde drama go even deeper: these plays question the efficiency of language as an instrument of genuine communication —so does the British school of linguistic philosophy. If Pinter's characters talk nonsense, because they use language loosely and emotively, that corresponds to the critique of language made by the philosophers concerned. If Beckett and Pinter fight shy of providing their characters with neat motivations, so does modern psychology, whether psycho-analytical or behaviouristic; for however widely these schools of psychology may diverge from each other, they agree about the immense difficulty of ever summing up a human being's motivations under any simple headings. And as to the unity of the characters, the consistency in the behaviour of a human being from the cradle to the grave—it may again be remarked that with the coming of modern psychological thought this concept (which ultimately derives from the Christian concept of an immortal soul, the unchanging *essence* of a human being) has lost much of its basis: each individual acts according to his situation at any given moment of his life and may change his personality as his circumstances, social, biological, psychological, change. And as to neat solutions of all problems, social, personal or ethical—again such solutions could only be provided in a society, a cultural climate in which a strongly established religious or ethical system provides all members of the society concerned with identical and generally accepted certainties. For good or ill, whether we like it or not, our Western society today lacks any such generally accepted system of ethics or philosophy. That is why contemporary drama merely raises questions, and refrains from providing solutions.

But—does this mean that the plays we have been discussing confront their audience with a message of unmitigated gloom and deep despair? I think it would be quite wrong to assume any such thing. True enough, playwrights like Beckett and Pinter confront us with the precariousness, the stark comfortlessness of the human condition; they remind us that we know little about our purpose in life and that there is no escape from the ravages of time and death. They hold out no illusion of social progress or compensation for our sufferings in an after-life. For those who cherish or depend on such beliefs, these dramatists are messengers of despair. But not for those others who feel that there is a dignity and a liberation in being able to live one's life without any cheap comforts such as those provided by consoling and unverifiable beliefs. For these people there is a higher degree of dignity and maturity in facing the human condition as it is with all its mystery, in the full knowledge that we have to go on living without ever knowing the ultimate truths of existence. This, after all, is the attitude that underlies the dominant philosophy of our times: the philosophy embodied in the basic assumptions of the natural sciences and their method. It is the very essence of the scientific attitude that nothing is ever certain, that we are surrounded by a vast wall of darkness in which we patiently make a breach here and there, but that each step forward opens up new vast areas of the unknown. To the scientist his awareness that he will never know all the mysteries of the universe, that the experimental results of today may well be invalidated by those of tomorrow, that there are no certainties and that all knowledge is fragmentary and fallible is no cause for despair. On the contrary: the very acceptance of these basic truths gives his endeavours their greatness and their dignity.

And so too the message of dramatists like Samuel Beckett and Harold Pinter is anything but gloomy or despairing. On the contrary: the starkness of their reminders of the evanescence of life and the certainty of death, their uncompromising rejection of any easy solution or cheap illusion of comfort ultimately has a liberating effect; such is the nature of man that in the very act of facing up to the reality of his condition his dignity is enhanced; we are only defeated by things by which we are taken unawares; what we know and have faced up to we can master. That is the reason why the effect of the plays we have discussed is anything but hopelessness or despair, why many of them ring with the laughter of their audiences, why tears and humour, the tragic and the comic, are equally present in this new kind of drama.

Drama with a Message: Arnold Wesker

by Laurence Kitchin

Future historians of mid-twentieth century drama will have to do a lot of homework on the political background, and I don't envy them the job. Stock responses along one or another political groove were the main obstacle to critical assessment of the new English playwrights who came to the front from 1956 onwards. The artistic vitality of this new wave came from an upsurge of attitudes, diction, and characters formerly unknown to our stage; but it seems that the release of energy among the supposedly inhibited English could only take place in the absence of genteel restraint. At all events, most of the new writers had an education well short of university standards. The result is a freshness of imaginative response side by side with conceptual poverty, as if they were artistically mature and intellectually virgin.

In many critical opponents of the New Wave this condition seemed to have been reversed. They knew well enough that Wesker's quarrelsome cooks, not to mention Jimmy Porter, were newcomers to the stage, bringing no joy to timid playgoers in search of reassurance. Yet when it came to dealing with the subversive message, the protest, these critics, some of them veterans reared on Shaw, shirked the issue and fell back on the snobbish formula 'kitchen sink'. Although they had the advantage over the dramatists in education and experience, they greeted the dramatic equivalent of a social revolution with vague gestures of distaste and never brought their

"Drama with a Message: Arnold Wesker" by Laurence Kitchin. From *Experimental Drama,* ed. W. A. Armstrong (London: G. Bell and Sons Ltd., 1963).

minds to bear on it. Honest and reasoned dismissiveness is one of the main functions of criticism. Why, with such an obvious cue for it, did so many abstain? Simply, I think, because they had long lost the habit of taking any living English playwright seriously; they had come to accept the West End image of drama as recreational only, and with it the divorce of our theatre from intellectual life.

Having failed to define the New Wave's admittedly meagre stock of ideas, its opponents went on to reveal an astonishing ignorance of dramatic form. They repeatedly invoked the Edwardian concept of a 'well made play' without, apparently, having broken down even that limited vehicle to its elements, which are in fact two or three star actors in scenes contrived for the display of personality and technique. Such parochialism, leaving out as it did most of the world drama's expressive range, including Shakespeare's method in the histories, was especially unsuited to coping with the new English work. The new playwrights were actively opposed to boulevard drama, and in Wesker's case any objection to it in principle was reinforced by total ignorance of it. Working as a kitchen porter in Paris, he never went to the theatre at all.

Only by trying to explain why the dismissive criticism was so inept can we fully grasp what a hopeless divergence there has been in this case between artistic intention and critical response. Unhappily, the new drama had to design most of its own critical apparatus as it went along. It's hardly surprising that partisans come out of it little better than the opposition; given little or no authoritative guidance, they grabbed anything within reach like an unarmed man in a riot. Hence the unhelpful use of 'anti-illusionism', 'menace', 'edge', 'epic' and a sense of 'commitment' as vague as the opposition's 'kitchen sink'. Most of this is the small change of theatrical history, and to appreciate Wesker as a playwright, it's only necessary to remember that his commitment to Socialism is a product of family background. Compared with the commitment of a Brecht, Miller, or Sartre, it is a sheltered position in time and place; but it has led Wesker to the heart of a problem which is occupying the full attention of greater minds than his. The context is the affluent society of the mid-century capitalist Western world and the problem is in the end moral and/or social. How is the underprivileged mass to become fully human? Wesker's solution, that of an artist rather than a moralist or propagandist, is roughly on the lines of E. M. Forster's 'only connect'. He believes that it can be done by education and the arts. This positive aspect of his drama distinguishes Wesker from other new-wave playwrights and from many other Socialists. It accounts for the inner coherence which controls his dramatic writing; but, in so far as the wiring system along which the benevolence travels is of Socialist pattern, commitment is at times a source of weakness.

Regarded strictly as a dramatist, as an audience would regard him without reference to his personal background, social significance, 'message' or mission, Wesker's most notable qualities are emotional maturity and his command of action in depth. The first means that he never condescends to his characters, the second that what happens on stage is always more interesting in performance than we would be likely to guess from quotation. In much 'literary' drama the reverse is true in both cases and causes a quick dismissal to the shelf, whereas *Roots* was immediately successful with provincial audiences. The contact is usually made without resorting to verbal artifice or strenuous theatrical effects. Under the surface of dialogue which, like O'Neill's, is often limp and colourless on the page, there comes into focus a network of relationships more significant than the interplay in the foreground, which can be written off as a quarrel between cooks or the gushing quotation of a half-educated young man's ideas, accurate but uninspiring. The inner framework, on the contrary, contains social and political issues, held together dramatically by the playwright's urgent concern for them and by his conviction that they affect the homely characters in front. Thus, behind Ronnie Kahn lies the Hungarian revolution of 1956 and behind both is the fact of the author's Russo-Hungarian descent; behind Peter the cook lies German idealism and violence; and behind Beatie Bryant is a generation faced with a new kind of choice. In each case there are three sources of pressure: current affairs, the author's attitude, and the characters in the play.

At the end of *Roots* there is a good example of the way this threefold pressure is applied. The elementary theatrical situation is that of a heroine ditched by her fiancé and alone with a family she has outgrown. From the current sociological angle, Beatie Bryant is a working-class girl, newly awakened to the joys of abstract painting, classical music, and extra-marital love. From Wesker's angle she is all that, and also a creature with a choice between self-realisation and absorption by the greedy mass of spenders corrupted by advertising; from her own, she is a woman in love who has done her best to reconcile her boy-friend's view of life with that of her mother. By the end of the play she has been let down by everybody, yet she chooses that moment to assert herself with all the zest of a woman who at last knows her own mind. It works, because the commonplace events on stage register a series of pressures beyond those undergone by the characters. From her mother's point of view, Beatie is an upstart, justly punished for claiming to know better than her elders. That, in fact, is the external stage picture, but it is not the picture we take away. We take away an experience summed up by Beatie's final statement, but arrived at through action working at such a depth that the fiancé, who has a major part in it, never puts in an appearance.

The habit of assigning new plays to categories, and responding accordingly, grows on critics during lean periods like the one which came to an end in 1956. Hence the tendency to approach *Roots* as a play with a dull first act, as an essay in Norfolk dialect, and so on, instead of paying close attention to what the play does.[1] *The Kitchen*, the first play he wrote, had a critical reception confused by this rigid approach, the more so because the novelty of its setting lent it a surface affinity with plays like *The Women*, *Counsellor-at-Law*, *Men in White*, and *You Won't Always be on Top* which leaned heavily on physical situation, ranging from a women's hairdresser's to a building site. How little the play's meaning depends on its documentation of catering behaviour can be seen by comparing any stage production of it with the film version, in which photographic realism weakens the effect. The play demands that we take in the whole cavernous place at a glance, that we enter into a unity of time, place, and action such as the theatre alone can offer. More important than the novelty of the setting is its apt scale, for it is the kitchen of a large restaurant and arouses the expectancy exerted by parade grounds, throne rooms, and similar spaces which

[1] Cf. John Mander, *The Writer and Commitment* (Secker and Warburg, 1961), for a meaningful analysis.

seem to await a crowd. We take our seats before the performance to find the curtain already raised on this space. 'The kitchen is always there', says the stage direction. Well, certainly the stage is, and it is waiting for something, though not for us. In this curious atmosphere the night porter gets up off the floor and lights the stove. Something has begun; and we have been made to expect more than a tour behind the scenes at a restaurant. Yet the play builds up to the question—'What is there more?'

The Kitchen was produced first, at the Royal Court in September, 1959, but only for members' performances on Sunday. *Roots* and *Chicken Soup with Barley* had already put its author on the map, but presumably *The Kitchen* was not thought to be good enough for the main bill and a normal run, open to the general public. However, it was staged again in November of the same year, this time by amateurs. 'That the Cambridge University Mummers', began a notice in *The Times,* 'should put on a play by an author still under thirty, whose education ended at the age theirs effectively began, may seem a curious twist of theatrical history.' After claiming for *The Kitchen* 'merits beyond the novelty of its setting' this notice went on: 'Indeed, the rhythm, depth of feeling, action, and characterisation, controlled in the service of a meaningful statement about the human condition, with the whole compressed into just over one hour, incline one, when these qualities also exert a continuous grip on the audience, to regard this as major drama.' [2]

If Wesker as a dramatist is to be weighed as seriously as that, and in the case of his first play, I think *The Kitchen* needs taking apart and some of its components laid out for inspection. Most of the dismissive reactions to the play so far have suffered from the restrictive notions about dramatic form which I have already tried to account for, as well as from the title's power to trigger off the stereotyped abusive epithet; and many favourable reactions have been limited to the lively surface effects, especially the lunch-hour crises, a director's delight with kitchen staff filling the stage and surging about like mad. Is there really anything more in all this than close observation of a sleazy environment, arbitrarily whipped into a crude approximation to drama from time to time? Many think not;

[2] *The Times* (November 19, 1959).

but what worries me about their attitude is a suspicion that they might think the same of *The Iceman Cometh* and *The Lower Depths.*

The Kitchen can be analysed at four levels: documentary, character, conflict, and total statement or resolution. After that it may be possible to appreciate its form, though not in terms of 'realism', 'naturalism', 'propaganda', or similar evasions of a look at the object itself, the play. Of the documentary aspect not much need be said. We see the work of the kitchen start up, rise to a climax in the mid-day rush, simmer down and rise to a climax again. Real time is telescoped, but can be accepted as more or less continuous, though there are two breaks, one after the first rush and another during the lull. To anyone familiar with Orwell's *Down and Out in Paris and London,* Marlowe's *Coming, Sir!* or service in the armed forces, nothing of great sociological interest is revealed. Wesker's experience of the work is a guarantee of authenticity, and that's about all. When it comes to character, we will be disappoinetd if we look for any great insight or complexity; there are too many of them and there is too little time. Moreover, not one of them develops, as Beatie Bryant does, or learns anything new from start to finish. These might appear to be crippling defects, were it not for the fact that the characters do take on independent life, mainly because they speak in varied accents and dialects. We get the flavour of distinct personalities from the brief incidents which detach them from the crowd. This has been taken too much for granted, and seems to me remarkably skilful. An obvious parallel is O'Neill's definition of his crowd in *The Iceman Cometh,* but he takes four times as long to do it. Wesker's people are less characters than personalities, indeed it is part of the statement that they are not characters, but as usual with him they refer to a social context far bigger than themselves, to boring work, misused leisure, incentives, retirement, and other subjects of mid-century anxiety or debate.

As for conflict, there is plenty of it in the endemic form of interracial and, so to speak, inter-departmental rivalry, dramatic only in a dispersed and fitful way, like demarcation disputes in industry. The main conflict is between Peter, the German cook, and the entire set-up. Even Peter is thinly characterised, in the sense that we learn nothing about his past and little about his present except that he is touchy, imaginative, idealistic, and in love, a captive Shelley preparing turbot and cod. But Peter is the only person out of more than thirty who has an urge to make sense of it all. He protests, but unlike Beatie he never arrives at giving his protest an intellectual sanction; so it destroys him. This conflict, between the *status quo,* the life sentence condemning the underprivileged to demoralising work, and a single personality, is blurred because Peter lives by impulse and is vulnerably romantic. Yet Wesker has chosen to pile all the pressures on him. All the resolution really amounts to is Peter's crack-up, followed by the proprietor's 'I don't know what more to give a man. He works, he eats, I give him money. This is life, isn't it?' The ironic finality of that needs to be sparked off by something more considered than Peter's collapse. Only at a rather facile theatrical level does the waste of Peter come across more urgently than the waste of his companions, but we could make the same complaint about Uncle Vanya. Although what happens to Peter is logical in the circumstances, the weight given to him distracts us from the predicament of the restaurant staff as a whole. The collective situation has been explored with such compassion that we resent the narrowing down of interest to a private case of hysteria at the climax.

The formal structure of the play is otherwise entirely satisfactory. A kitchen on stage can be accepted as a Capitalist microcosm with the proprietor standing in for God. The relationships and conflicts resemble those in other industries enough to prevent the documentary aspect from obscuring the point. First we are introduced to the people and, rare in the theatre, their work. Then they are shown under stress. In the subsequent lull a few of them go as far as they can towards reflecting on their situation. Finally, there is the feverish progress to an overwhelming question. The contours of significant action rise to the break period, structurally a climax though subdued in tone. I am plotting the inner action; the usual critical method would mark the lunch-hour rush as a climax and the break period as a relaxation, merely because one is noisy and the other quiet. In fact the reverse is true. The core of the play is a conversation in which Peter asks five of the others what they want from life. One wants tools and gadgets, the second sleep, the third money, the fourth women, the fifth human understanding. When the same question is put to Peter himself, he doesn't answer, or rather he answers in character by forgetting that the question has been asked. He has just caught sight of Monique, the waitress he is in love with. This wonderful scene, with the ovens at half-power, a guitar playing, and men of limited intellect fumbling with the issues which convulse the mid-century world, is a masterpiece by any standard. In the formal scheme it comments on what has gone before and enriches the seemingly trivial conflicts before and after. It recalls in various ways O'Neill, Gorki, and Chekhov.

Finally, we return to another work episode, at first with some slackening of tension, since the novelty of the setting has worn off. The action is soon climbing steeply to Peter's crack-up. Whatever we may think about its effect on the total statement, it isn't, as many have claimed, arbitrary or 'unexpected'.[3] In fact you can plot a graph of the collapse by numbers on the script: (1) the chef threatens to sack Peter for giving cutlets to a tramp, (2) Peter says he can't dream in a kitchen, (3) Monique refuses to elope with him because her husband has bought a house, and (4) during a demarcation dispute a waitress calls him a Bosch and a bloody German bastard. Anyone surprised when Peter blows his top at this point cannot have understood what's been going on or have remembered that before his first entrance he has been linked with violence.

All the same, Peter's place in the scheme remains a debating point, because the scheme itself is so good. Two lines of defence, neither of them wholly convincing, can be followed. One is to take him as an essay in expressionist violence, an instrument registering the extremes of conflict elsewhere stated through people whose interest is limited by apathy or brutish prejudice. If working-class drama is to be more than reporting, at least one character must be given insight enough to lend events a shape. It would be cheating in this environment to introduce the necessary factor on an intellectual plane, so it is done emotionally instead, by the presence of a sensibility unstable but superior. The other artistic defence of Peter would be to adapt Kedrov's dictum that *Uncle Vanya* is an orchestra of which Vanya is the 'cello, to call Peter the solo instrument in a concerto. Either way, Peter is an impressive creation with

[3] Alan Pryce-Jones, *New English Dramatists, 2* (Penguin Books, 1960).

the special appeal of characters who seem to break out of a play's design and take on independent life. As a part he might become a challenge to distinguished actors.

Wesker's claim to serious critical attention can very well rest on *The Kitchen* and *Roots*. I have tried to explain the dramatic strength of *Roots* elsewhere.[4] It is the middle play in a trilogy starting with *Chicken Soup with Barley* and completed by *I'm talking about Jerusalem*, less well received than the other two plays. Rather than discuss the trilogy before it has been put to the test by being acted as such on one day, I'd now like briefly to underline the maturity of *Chicken Soup with Barley*. I have a suspicion that the play's muted impact in the theatre may have been a result of inhibited presentation, that it could stand up to very tight interplay and solo work on a big scale. In short, I would like to see Method actors, plus Katina Paxinou, let loose on it. Otherwise the playwright who invented Peter can seem in his second play to be holding something back.

Even under restraint, the feeling which governs *Chicken Soup with Barley* is remarkably mature. There are three acts, in 1936, 1946, and 1956. The action is that of time, politics, and social change on a Jewish East End family, the Kahns; and one way to appreciate it is to imagine what a mess this or that other 'committed' playwright would be likely to make of the same subject. The route is littered with invitations to get lost, as, say, Osborne does, in a piquant stage relationship or lay down the law at political slogan level. Instead of that, the political issues are almost inseparable from Wesker's characters and seem as much a part of the household as a cup of tea. For example, the change of socialist climate from the militancy of 1936 to the post-war realism of ten years later is pointed by Sarah Kahn's, 'Ah, Harry, you couldn't even make money during the war. The war! When *everybody* made money'. It is done without having her step a fraction out of character or her nagging role in the relationship. Ten years later it is Sarah again who raises a major issue. *The Kitchen's* 'what is there more?' theme has just been re-stated, and very precisely. 'There's nothing more to life than a house, some friends, and a family,' Monty says.

[4] *Mid-Century Drama* (Faber, 1960).

'And when someone drops an atom bomb on your family?' Sarah demands. But she never dwindles to a mouthpiece for opinions; politics is only one element in the showdown between herself and her son which ends the play.

Ronnie touches it off by saying, 'You're a pathological case, Mother . . . You're still a *communist!*' We are in late 1956, with Ronnie's faith in mankind torn to shreds by the Soviet Union's repressive action in Hungary, the last straw in a multiple process of disillusionment. From Sarah's answer it emerges that her enemy is less Capitalism than apathy. She enables us to view apathy in precise terms. It is the worker's contentment with possessing a television set; it is nihilism and the philosophy of the absurd; it is her feckless husband, Harry; and here and now it is her son, sunk in despair. The play has shown it spreading relentlessly over this little community. It is the Death Wish, contested at this point only by Sarah's pig-headed dislike of people in authority and faith in an idea of brotherhood. 'Ronnie,' she finishes, 'if you don't care you'll die.'

Although he arrives there with greatly inferior intellectual equipment and totally different techniques, Wesker reaches commanding heights from which he is able to ask questions as urgent as those asked by Shaw. He has the advantage over Shaw in emotional maturity and at times in the layers of meaning piled up behind external action. We could follow other characters, like Ronnie, Ada, or Harry, in and out of *Chicken Soup with Barley* and find them as accurately fixed as Sarah in the context of home, neighbourhood, and politics. Art as well organised as this will not yield its full flavour to criticism fettered by political opinion, Right or Left, still less to over-simplified notions of dramatic form.

Finally, something needs to be said about Wesker's relationship to the new movement in the English theatre, which first made itself felt in 1956. Here I am only concerned with it in so far as it might affect his own development. Where he shares its characteristics, he tends also to be distinct from it, as a result of superior maturity and insight. This can be seen by comparing his handling of, say, conflict between parents and children, social protest, violence or a working-class milieu, with that of other young playwrights. But Wesker's theatrical idiom, the entire flavour of his work in performance, sets him aside from boulevard drama and the show-business *status quo*. He arrived as a candidate for study at University level without having had a West End success. It has been made possible by a revolutionary situation which split the English theatre into two almost irreconciliable camps. Not only was Wesker's drama asserted mainly outside the traditional institutions of the London theatre, but the starting-point of it was unorthodox. Instead of serving an apprenticeship to accepted ideas of craftsmanship, he drew his inspiration from the London School of Film Technique. Indeed, he regards his innocence of technical dogma as an advantage, which permitted him to construct in terms of thirty-two characters, ovens on stage, or three acts timed at intervals of ten years.

Inevitably, though, this approach is likely to expose Wesker more and more to the New Wave's taste in stage presentation, including its tendency to play down the spoken word, emphasise vigorous action and reduce the playwright's status to membership of a team.[5] Brecht, a genius both as writer and director, could afford to accept this democratic subordination in principle; for other dramatists, as we have seen, it can be dangerous. Wesker has stated: 'I am working very much towards a reduction not only of scenery, but of dialogue as well. I am becoming more conscious of style, and I bet the rest of my plays are no bloody good. The less I say, the better I like it. This, I think, is the result not so much of my interest in cinematic forms, as of working in the theatre, talking to other playwrights, and becoming aware, more and more aware that the theatre is a place where one wants to *see* things happening.' [6]

Well, that isn't an attitude entirely to be welcomed in a dramatist with such a supple and unobtrusive mastery of the spoken word. But sooner or later the playwright must come to grips with the production techniques of his time, must take what serves his purpose and disregard the rest. The choice will be made under heavy pressure from technical enthusiasts, but it is finally up to him. Wesker's problem will be to come out of the grapple without loss of artistic identity. The success of *Chips with Everything* illustrates this vividly. Audiences are gripped by the savage precision of military training, by rebellious dancing and singing at a canteen party. They remember the raid on the coke store, which is indebted to a

[5] *Chips with Everything.*
[6] *Twentieth Century,* February, 1961.

similar episode in *West Side Story*. And all these effects depend at least as much on John Dexter's brilliant direction as on anything given by the dramatist. In the new idiom, Wesker's characterisation is sometimes sketchy where one would least expect it, among the working-class victims; and the public school man trying to identify himself with them is outside Wesker's range. So this is a transitional work, flawed in the process of releasing extra power. Perhaps the flaws have helped to make the play a commercial success. It is essentially an attack on the British 'ruling class', symbolised by R.A.F. officers. As such it is the most powerfully subversive drama to have been welcomed as entertainment within living memory.

John Arden

by John Russell Taylor

Perhaps the biggest single thing to stand in the English Stage Company's favour, whenever and wherever these things finally come to be totted up, will be their continued championship of John Arden in the face of a Press dubious to hostile and of almost complete public apathy (his three plays to be performed publicly at the Royal Court have achieved in all a mere seventy-three performances). And in this perseverance they have been absolutely right, as more and more people, both among the critics and among the theatre-going public, are coming to recognize. All the same, the hostility and plain indifference manifested by the vast majority of the plays' first spectators is quite easy to understand; one could even understand why many not properly attuned to Arden's work should find it downright boring. The explanation resides in one fact, simple in itself but extremely complex in its implications: Arden's view of his characters and situations is in effect the most unflinchingly amoral in the British theatre today.

Not immoral; that would be shocking (even now, since conventions still rule even where convictions have flagged), it would be 'provocative', and most important of all it would imply by categorically rejecting certain standards that these standards nevertheless existed—there would still be clear, dramatic blacks and whites, even if they did not always come in the expected places. But amorality is something very different: we can stand a little uncertainty about which are our heroes and which are our villains, but where

"John Arden" by John Russell Taylor. From *Anger and After: A Guide to the New British Drama* (London: Methuen & Co. Ltd., 1962); also published as *The Angry Theater* (New York: Hill & Wang, Inc., 1962).

do we stand in a situation which seems to deny the very possibility of heroism or villainy? The question may not be all that worrying on a purely personal level—one could argue that such concepts as heroism and villainy have little meaning in Pinter's work, for example—but Arden brings us face to face with it in its baldest form by embodying his attitudes in plays which appear to be about general social, moral, and political issues: colour prejudice and prostitution, social clashes on a housing estate, pacifism, the treatment of old age.

For behind Arden's work there seems to be brooding one basic principle: not exactly the obvious one that today there are no causes—that would be altogether too facile, and in any case just not true—but that there are too many. There are as many causes as there are people (more, since many are quite capable of espousing two or more mutually exclusive causes at the same time), and only the naïve can suppose that any two people who are, say, pacifists (to choose a nice, convenient label) will believe the same things for the same reasons. In other words, in all Arden's plays the characters we meet are first and foremost just people: not concepts cast into a vaguely human mould, with built-in labels saying 'good' or 'bad', 'hero' or 'villain', to help us into the right grooves. (Arden himself in an interview has expressed 'grave objections to being presented with a character on the stage whom you know to be the author's mouthpiece' and said that he 'cannot see why a social play should not be so designed that we may find ourselves understanding the person's problems, but not necessarily approving his reactions to them'.)

It follows, therefore, that the behaviour of any one person or group does not imply any general judgment. *The Waters of Babylon* is not a play in favour of prostitution and tenant-exploitation (or for that matter the reverse); *Live Like Pigs* tells us nothing about 'The Welfare State'; *Serjeant Musgrave's Dance* is not for or against pacifism *per se; The Happy Haven* offers no solution to the problem of old age: they are just plays about individual people affected one way or another by these issues. Hence, perhaps—until one gets used to Arden's way of seeing things at least—the confusion and irritation of his audiences: when 'parity of esteem' for all the characters is pushed so far, identification and taking sides become difficult if not impossible, and though undeniably the characters conflict—they are conflicting all the time—for many theatregoers a conflict in which they are not asked themselves to participate is in effect no conflict at all; left rudderless and all at sea, they end up lost and bored.

This happened in its most extreme form, to judge from the notices anyway, with his first professionally staged play, *The Waters of Babylon,* and with his recent *The Happy Haven.* At the time *The Waters of Babylon* was put on for one Sunday night production-without-décor at the Royal Court, Arden was still a practising architect (he was born in Barnsley in 1930, educated partly at state, partly at public schools, and studied architecture at Cambridge and Edinburgh); he had written various plays in verse or prose (including a schoolboy effort 'on the death of Hitler written in the style of *Samson Agonistes*' and 'a pseudo-Elizabethan tragedy on the Gunpowder Plot, which was very bad, a sort of academic play in verse'), had a period comedy about the building of a railway called *All Fall Down* (which he compares with Whiting's *Penny for a Song*) performed by fellow students at Edinburgh, and won a B.B.C. Northern Region prize for his radio play *The Life of Man.* This, which he calls 'a sort of seafaring thing' with 'a little too much of *Moby Dick* in it', attracted the attention of the Royal Court, and though they rejected the first play he submitted (based on an Arthurian legend), they accepted *The Waters of Babylon* as the first of their low-budget Sunday-night ventures.

In general the critics did not think much of it, and without agreeing with them one can easily see why: it is in many ways the most teasing and apparently perverse of all his plays in what it says (or appears to be saying), even apart from the eccentricity of its form and style. Briefly, its central character, its 'hero' if you like, is a Polish émigré who leads a double life, working in an architect's office by day while out of office hours he runs a lodging-house occupied by eighty exploited foreign tenants and a number of the string of prostitutes he 'manages'. Worse, he claims to have been in Buchenwald, and so he was, but as a member of the German army. And yet in spite of all this he is certainly the most sympathetically delineated character, in most respects amiable, good-natured and thoroughly likeable; and so indeed are the prostitutes and ex-prostitutes, with whom his relations are of the friendliest. If we start lining up characters and concepts, as many of the play's first audience did, we shall be forced to some very odd conclusions. But that, clearly, is not Arden's intention; instead he gives us a picturesque mixture of comedy and a little drama as Krank (Sigismanfred Krankiewicz) tries desperately to raise the money to pay off a patriotic fellow Pole who is setting up a bomb plot in his lodging-house by rigging, with the aid of 'Uncle Charlie' Butterthwaite, erstwhile 'Napoleon of Local Government', the results of a new municipal lottery (the play began as a satire on the Premium Bond system). There are really no heroes and no villains; Krank is quite sympathetic, but too contradictory and elusive to be really heroic, the girls and the crooks are mostly likeable, while even their obvious opponents—the straight negro [sic] councillor Joseph Caligula, the fatuous M. P. Loap, and the shifty chauvinist Henry Ginger—are too complicated to stand, singly or together, as villains.

Worse still, for an already sufficiently puzzled audience, the style in which this mystifying confection is written offers manifold complexities in itself. Some of the dialogue is written in a springy, colloquial, realistic style, some, particularly the maliciously accurate parodies of the Hyde Park orators' styles, suggests that satire is intended, some, especially Krank's monologues, is written in a fairly highly wrought free verse, and to make matters worse several of the characters have a disconcerting habit of bursting into song at odd moments. Indeed, were it not for the life and vigour of the whole thing, its tremendous theatrical drive and panache, the brisk conclusion of most reviewers that 'this young man may have ideas but cannot begin to put them together into a play' might be comprehensible, if not quite forgivable.

Not quite forgivable because, even apart from the evident and abundant life of the play, Arden does at one point come unusually close to a direct statement of what he is at, and an attentive ear should not have missed it. In the last act Paul, the patriot, is berating Krank for his war record; 'We know what you were', he cries. Krank turns on him:

> But I don't know what *you* are. Or you, Henry Ginger.
> Or all the rest of you, with your pistols and your orations,
> And your bombs in your private house, and your fury,

And your national pride and honour. This is the lunacy.
This was the cause, the carrying through of all that insensate war,
  This is the rage and purposed madness of your lives,
That *I,* Krank, do not know. I *will* not know it,
Because, if I know it, from that light day forward,
I am a man of time, place, society and accident;
Which is what I must not be. Do you understand me . . . ?
The world is running mad in every direction,
It is quicksilver, shattered, here, here, here, here.
All over the floor. Go on, hustle after it,
Chase it, dear Paul. But I choose to follow
Only such fragments as I can easily catch.
I catch them, I keep them such time as I choose,
Then roll them away down and follow another.
Is that philosophy? It is a reason anyway. . . .

In all his plays Arden has chosen to do just this, to follow only such fragments as he can easily catch, catch them, keep them such time as he chooses, then roll them away and follow others; his world is shattered, like ours, and the plays he has made out of it are comprehensible only if considered as certain fragments selected, isolated and shaped into a whole; what we must not do is to assume that they are microcosms of a complete, coherent world, and then seek to read its character in their various faces.

This becomes even more evident when Arden's next two plays, *Soldier, Soldier* and *Live Like Pigs* (*Soldier, Soldier* was actually written first, for B.B.C. Television, but not produced until two years later), are taken into consideration. For in them the style already in the making in *The Waters of Babylon* emerges fully fledged, and the affinities of this style as well as the subject-matter it is used on enforce a more detailed consideration both of Arden's style and of his intentions. The name most frequently evoked in connexion with Arden's work is that of Brecht, and the affinity is certainly there. Arden, paradoxically, is at once the most and the least Brechtian of all modern British dramatists: most, because their views on the proper relationship between the audience and what is happening on stage and their means of achieving it are almost identical; least, because one could readily imagine that Arden's plays would have been written in exactly the same way if Brecht had never existed. Basic to Arden's drama is something strikingly akin to

Brecht's celebrated A-effect: as we have remarked already, though there are all sorts of conflicts taking place on stage, the audience is never invited to participate in them; it is even forcibly prevented on occasion from doing so. Instead it is invited to experience the play as a self-contained totality, and to judge—though on a human level rather than in terms of general concepts (herein lies the vital difference between Arden's practice and Brecht's theory, though, of course, Brecht's practice is a good deal nearer to Arden than his theory would lead one to expect).

This is achieved largely through an unashamed and deliberate resort to 'theatricality', to various formal devices which keep the viewer constantly aware that he is in a theatre (or in front of a television screen) watching a *play.* Song plays an important part in Arden's work, and is used almost always quite non-realistically: anyone may express him- or herself in song, usually song closely related in form and style to the English folksong and ballad. So, too, with passages of heightened speech in rhyme or sometimes in free verse which is still appreciably verse rather than prose: indeed, in Arden's later plays the distinction between verse and prose has become more marked, and he now finds passages in the earliest plays in which such a distinction is not clearly made muzzy and unsatisfactory. He says, for instance, of *The Waters of Babylon,* where there is a lot of verse;

> I feel on re-reading it that many of the scenes would have been better if I had gone about it more naturalistically, and used a more natural prose. I think the use of formal verse and straightforward vernacular prose in juxtaposition is quite a good solution even in a modern play. If people are speaking formal verse with lines that rhyme, the audience does not have to worry whether it sounds natural or not. They are talking poetry. It's with the half-and-half thing that one is in trouble.

And what sort of subject-matter is the critical detachment achieved in this way to be applied to? In both *Soldier, Soldier* and *Live Like Pigs* to evidently 'social' subjects, since in each case we witness an unsettling incursion of uncontrollable outside forces into a hitherto settled community. The only trouble, from a conventional viewpoint, is deciding which side we should be on, that of the intruder or that of the intruded upon. Either, our preconceptions would lead us to suppose, the dramatist must be for order, authority and all the rest of it and against the forces of anarchy and disorder, or he must be against established complacency and for those who rebel against it. But somehow neither of these neat theorizations seems to work in either case. In the first the Soldier, an obvious bad lot, lies and cheats his way into the household of another soldier missing from his regiment, pretending he knows the boy and that he alone can extract him from some terrible trouble he has fallen into; he proceeds to bleed the family dry, seduce the son's wife, and make off with as much of their savings as he can conveniently extract. So, surely, we should be against him and for his victims. But no, not a bit of it; like Krank, this 'randy chancer' is strangely likeable; there is certainly something fetching about his all-out way of life. But on the other hand the Scuffhams, his victims, are not presented as in any way villains of hypocrisy and complacency who deserve all they get; they are not very bright, admittedly, but they might fairly be described, like the Jacksons in *Live Like Pigs,* as 'undistinguished but not contemptible'.

Their situation, in fact, is in many ways identical with that of the Jacksons, a cosy conventional family happy in their housing-estate semi-detached until the Sawneys, a wild and disreputable family of near-gipsies, are moved protesting into the house next door. But in *Live Like Pigs,* since a political question (for or against the Welfare State?) appears to be involved, the issue of allegiances is even more acute. On this subject one can hardly do better than quote from Arden's own Introductory Note to the printed text:

> On the one hand, I was accused by the Left of attacking the Welfare State: on the other, the play was *hailed* as a defence of anarchy and amorality. So perhaps I had better declare myself. I approve outright neither of the Sawneys nor of the Jacksons. Both groups uphold standards of conduct which are incompatible, but which are both valid in their correct context.
>
> The Sawneys are an anachronism. They are the direct descendants of the 'sturdy beggars' of the sixteenth century, and the apparent chaos of their lives becomes an ordered pattern when seen in terms of a wild empty countryside and a nomadic existence. Put out of their fields by enclosing landlords, they found such an existence possible

for four hundred years. Today, quite simply, there are too many buildings in Britain, and there is just no room for nomads. The family in this play fails to understand this, and becomes educated in what is known as the 'hard way', but which might also be called the 'inefficient way'.

The Jacksons are an undistinguished but not contemptible family, whose comparative cosiness is not strong enough to withstand the violent irruption into their affairs that the Sawneys bring. Their natural instincts of decency and kindliness have never been subjected to a very severe test. When they are, they collapse. I do not regard them as being necessarily typical in this. They are the people I have chosen for the play, because they illustrate my theme in a fairly extreme form.

This passage has been worth quoting at length, because it is absolutely central to the full comprehension of Arden's methods and intentions. It makes it clear that his attitude to his creations is quite uncommitted; this means that, for instance, he does not defend the amorality of one group of characters nor, on the other hand, does he condemn it—they are individuals, and there are reasons, valid reasons, why they live as they do, even if they are displaced persons in the modern world. Similarly he does not condemn the very different standards of the Jacksons; they, too, have their reasons. He does not even seek to generalize from them about the behaviour of this *sort* of family; they also are individuals, just the people the dramatist has chosen for this particular play, and in doing so he, too, had his reasons.

Both *Soldier, Soldier* and *Live Like Pigs* achieved, despite and at least partly because of the initial misunderstandings, a modest measure of success (*Soldier, Soldier* even won the Italia Prize, thus laying to rest the B.B.C.'s doubts sufficiently for them to commission another play from Arden on the strength of it). But then both productions stressed the realistic elements at the expense of the others and tended if anything to underplay the comedy; in any case, they made the plays seem considerably more normal than *The Waters of Babylon*. But with his next play, *Serjeant Musgrave's Dance* (1959), Arden made a break with realism as it is generally understood on the English stage too decisive to be so easily smoothed over. As it happened, this appears to have made his style all the more acceptable (perhaps because playgoers still find it easier to take poetry and song in period drama than in a modern setting) and the play is in some intangible way his best known and most successful to date—'intangible' because on the stage it did little better than the others (twenty-eight performances to twenty-three of *Live Like Pigs* and twenty-two of *The Happy Haven*), but somehow it is the play of his that everyone seems to have heard of; it is revived by amateurs from time to time and the printed text continues to sell steadily.

The plot concerns the arrival of a group of deserters, led by Serjeant Musgrave, in a northern town in the 1880s, ostensibly recruiting but actually to teach the townfolk a lesson about war. In the town they are mistrusted at first—there are troubles at the mine and everyone equates soldiers with strike-breakers—but a little free beer gains them the amiability, if not exactly the friendship and confidence, of the miners, the mine-owner and his minions see the bit of colour and excitement offered by an all-out recruiting campaign a good thing to keep the workers occupied, and though one of the soldiers gets more or less accidentally killed in a struggle when the day of the meeting comes Musgrave is able to unfold his ideas to an audience initially ready and willing to receive them. But before long he has shocked them by revealing that in one of the boxes he has brought are the bones of a local boy, killed during the occupation of a foreign land; in reprisals five natives were killed for him, so now with the inexorable arithmetic of military logic Musgrave has decided that this five must again be multiplied by five to produce the number of those in authority who must be killed so that the lesson on the horrors of war will be well and truly learnt. Here his supporters start wavering; this is not what they had expected and one at least has believed their mission to be against killing *per se*. In the confusion the dragoons arrive, the soldiers are disarmed, and the miners, some of them happily forgetful of what is being enacted in front of them, others compelled by the presence of the army to join in, dance to celebrate the re-establishment of law and order.

This, even from such a bald summary, is obviously a very complex play, and again one must beware of confusing characters with concepts. At the time it was often found confusing because the liberal spectator saw in it a tract about pacifism which seemed to show that pacifism did not work; for the naïve this was simply because Musgrave and his men are defeated at the end; for the more perceptive because the motives and methods of the soldiers are so at odds with each other and often so apparently wrong-headed that it might be interpreted as an attempt to discredit pacifism by descrediting pacifists. Either Arden is for the pacifists, the argument would run, or he is against them, but if he is for them why has he not made them largely creditable and heroic, while if he is against them why has he made their opponents so discreditable and unheroic? Now there seems little doubt from what we know of Arden's personal views and what he has told us of the play's origins (the general concept of the town taken over from an American film by Hugo Fregonese, *The Raid*; the specific atrocity which inspires Musgrave's crusade from a parallel occurrence in Cyprus) that his sympathies are with the pacifists, yet clearly all his instincts as a dramatist prevent him from siding unequivocally with anyone; though the Parson and the Mayor come perhaps closer to hostile caricatures than any of his other characters, it is evident throughout that this is a play about individual, complicated human beings, and any simple alignment of character and concept is doomed to failure.

Musgrave himself, for instance, is right and sympathetic in his outrage at the atrocities which have been perpetrated abroad, but his decision that they can be expiated and a clean start be made only by a further shedding of blood is clearly much open to doubt; his 'logic' of order and discipline is inhuman and fails to take the natural way of things into account. From any point of view except one he is to blame for his blindness in supposing, as Mrs Hitchcock puts it in the last scene, that at the end of the world he could call a parade, and work everything out like a neat abstract geometrical progression; he is to blame for seeing life and love as a scribble on the neatly drawn, black-and-white plan of duty, rather than as the constants in terms of which any scheme of life must be drawn up. Unless, of course—and this is the one alternative—he is right when he says that God is with him; that he really is the representative of divine and by definition 'inhuman' justice that he believes himself to be. This point of view could be argued, but Arden does not here, any more than elsewhere, take sides; the idea serves simply to give coherence and a context to Musgrave's attitudes and help to explain why he is right in his terms just as Mrs Hitchcock is in hers, Attercliffe, the completely non-violent soldier, in his, and the dragoons no doubt in theirs (in an interview Arden has said himself that at the end 'law and order have been re-established by force; which, if you like, is the natural result of Musgrave trying to establish the opposite by force').

Formally *Serjeant Musgrave's Dance* is one of Arden's most successful pieces, the mature expression of the theme of *Soldier, Soldier* and, in a different way, of *Live Like Pigs*: the sudden explosive incursion of the extraordinary and disruptive into the normal and fairly orderly. It has a very slow and elaborate exposition, setting the scene and building up the situation to the climactic burst of violent action, and the songs and passages of heightened speech are integrated more effectively than ever before into the structure as a whole—already the separation between formal and colloquial is becoming more clear cut and decisive. The move towards at once greater formality of presentation and greater clarity and simplicity of expression seen here in its initial stages was to find a more extreme expression in his next theatrical play, *The Happy Haven* (1960-61), but meanwhile he wrote *A Christmas Play* for the church of Brent Knoll, the Somerset village where he was living at the time. Of this there is little to say except that it is of a radiant grace and simplicity which make clear some of the lessons Arden has learnt from a study of the medieval stage and its techniques, and that its depiction of Herod is so sympathetic that one or two critics have been tempted to write about it as a nativity play in which Herod is the hero. This is, of course, a journalistic oversimplification, but it reflects the fact that even here Arden is not ready to paint in unmistakable blacks and whites; Herod may not receive more than his due, but what is due to him he receives in full, and his actions are placed clearly in their historical-political context so that we can see that he was not a monster but just someone acting reasonably and with excellent intentions within the limitations of his own rule of conduct—the extreme case perhaps, of 'understanding the person's problems, but not necessarily approving his reactions to them'?

The Happy Haven, which Arden worked upon during his year as Drama Fellow at Bristol University and first produced there on an open stage, probably created a greater trouble in the breasts of the critics than any of his other plays when it reached the Royal

Court in 1961. The things which worried them were (*a*) that all the characters wear masks of some sort at some stage in the production, and most of them do so throughout; (*b*) that this is a comedy (Arden calls it a 'pantomime') about old people in an old folks' home. This meant to most critics that it was (*a*) crankily experimental and (*b*) a joke in bad taste. Both of which conclusions are distinctly curious. As far as the masks are concerned, there are excellent practical reasons for them, which Arden details in the *Encore* interview already quoted, among them mainly the advantages of using young actors so that the play is not slowed down and any too close realism which might incur the charge of cruelty is avoided. This charge has nevertheless been made; indeed, it is the basis of the assertion that the play is a joke in bad taste. But here we are back at the old trouble which has dogged us in any consideration of Arden's work, the confusion of characters with concepts. Certainly the old people are not represented as sweet, amiable, harmless old souls, ever ready with proverbial wisdom and tearful smiles of gratitude for any small attention which is shown them; instead, they are idiosyncratic human beings of distinct and complex temperaments (in itself perhaps a criticism to those who choose to believe that anyone over 70 must automatically become a depersonalized plaster saint). Arden chooses to tell the truth about old age, the unsentimental truth, summed up in Mrs Phineus's great speech in the third act, and sentimentalists do not like it:

> I'm an old lady
> And I don't have long to live.
> I am only strong enough to take
> Not to give. No time left to give.
> I want to drink, I want to eat,
> I want my shoes taken off my feet.
> I want to talk but not to walk
> Because if I walk, I have to know
> Where it is I want to go.
> I want to sleep but not to dream
> I want to play and win every game
> To live with love but not to love
> The world to move but me not move
> I want I want for ever and ever.

> The world to work, the world to be clever.
> Leave me be, but don't leave me alone.
> That's what I want. I'm a big round stone
> Sitting in the middle of a thunderstorm. . . .

But even supposing that this sort of attitude reflects discredit on the characters in the play—though surely the whole form in which it is cast, not to say its unmistakable humanity, forbids us to suppose so—and admitting that they show themselves in general quite capable of behaving just as badly as anyone else, what then? Does this make it an attack on old age itself? One would have to be pretty obtuse to think so. In fact, the plot of the play makes it, if we may assign any single moral to Arden for a moment, something much more like a plea for the old: an urging that they, too, are human beings and should be treated as such. Of course, such a schematic reading cannot be pushed too far—that is not Arden's way—but it has at least as much truth as the 'bad taste' view of the piece.

If it were the complete explanation, of course, the doctor who treats his patients as so many guinea-pigs would have to be the villain, but though he has been firmly pigeon-holed as such, notably by Mr Tom Milne in the *New Left Review,* this also is oversimplifying. Dr Copperthwaite, too, is acting with the best intentions; he, too, is in the right according to his own standards, and really sees his new youth elixir as a benefit to mankind, even if, carried away by his fanaticism on this subject he forgets to consider the feelings of the individual men and women in his charge, whom he intends to dose experimentally with the liquid. Indeed, whenever we seem at all in danger of seeing him too completely as the near-monster he becomes to the patients Arden devises a quick change of focus to help us see him in a far other and less intimidating light. For he is a weekend football player, and with his outside friends just an ordinary, undistinguished, rather juvenile young man. One of the patients, Mrs Letouzel, actually points out that this is so:

> He's the undisputed custodian of everything that's good for us. Security. Reliability. Though some people have said he failed to save the score the other Saturday at football. They relied on him to stop the goals, when he came back from the match he was swearing, frustrated—I know because I heard him. He'd let them through, he had to apolo-

> gize, I tell you I heard him. Apologized—Copperthwaite—in his humility, to the Captain of the Team. . . . But despite that, you silly children, we are all his worms. And he says 'Turn, worms, turn', and he thinks we have got no choice!

But we see and hear it ourselves; just at the moment when he has made his big discovery he has a phone conversation with the captain of the football team, full of fourth-form humour about 'medical goods—plain envelopes' and schoolboy jollity, while later he has an equally revealing conversation with his mother, who is slyly trying to introduce him, rather against his will, to eligible young women. Mr Milne is very hard on the first speech, finding that 'an important point is being made in this apparent digression: at a moment which may radically affect a number of people's lives, the doctor can respond only with prep-school smut and a sense of responsibility which treats people as no more than guinea-pigs. Never *stated,* this point is inescapable if viewed in its proper context.' Now there may well be some truth in this, but it seems to be reading at once too much and too little into the lines. The moral judgement is too lofty, really, since if the speech does not show the doctor in a particularly flattering light, at least it suggests that by any but a rigidly puritanical standard he is, out of office hours and seen for once through the eyes of someone other than his patients, a fairly normal, not specially bright or mature sort of chap—a point which emerges even more forcefully in the even more apparent digression of his conversation with his mother. In other words, like almost all Arden's other characters he is not a two-dimensional stereotype representing some abstract concept, but a human being with certain standards: we can understand his problems, even if we do not necessarily approve of his reactions to them.

Arden's course up to now has been as unpredictable as any in the British theatre, and it is anybody's guess what he will do next. After the extreme formalism of *The Happy Haven* he chose in his next play, the television piece *Wet Fish,* to go to the other extreme with a closer approach to naturalism than he had yet attempted, reducing the role of rhymed or appreciably formal verse to two short songs assigned to an evidently eccentric and in any case 'unEnglish' character. This latter turned out to be none other than our old friend Krank from *The Waters of Babylon,* complete with double life of architect's office by day and brothel-organization by night (not to mention Teresa at the other end of a phone and Alderman Charlie Butterthwaite rumbling in the distance). This time, however, we are shown mostly his 'respectable' life at work, since the office and the various jobs it has on hand—particularly the reconstruction of a fish shop for a friend of the architect—provide the play's principal material. Gathered into less than an hour and a half we have a tragi-comedy about the shop itself, the odd and intricate business-cum-romantic life of Krank, the initiation of a new female architect into business practice, some jiggery-pokery with the local council over new planning in the town, and quite a bit of semi-documentary stuff about the way an architect's office works. The result is rather a ragbag, but a lively one, bursting all over with scenes and strands of good plays which do not quite, in the end, hold together, but at least this prodigality of material is a fault on the right side.

Next on the horizon are *Ironhand,* a translation-adaption of Goethe's early play *Goetz von Berlichingen* commissioned by the Stratford Company for the Aldwych, and *The Workhouse Donkey,* a new play which the author describes as 'a vulgar melodrama', for the Royal Court. One thing seems certain, though: difficult though Arden's vision may be to accept on first acquaintance, and puzzling his way of expressing it, familiarity makes the approach much easier and breeds nothing but respect and admiration. John Arden is one of our few complete originals, and for the occasional faults in his plays—a desire to force a gallon into a pint pot, a tendency perhaps to overdo the gusty, gutsy side of things just a little from time to time—there are numerous and irreplaceable merits. Sooner or later his definitive success with a wider public is assured.

Arden's Stagecraft

by Albert Hunt

A soldier stands at the front of the stage. He is tall, upstanding, rigid—a dominating figure. When he speaks, his voice is powerful and commanding. He clasps his hands across his chest and begins to pray.

> God, my Lord God. Have You or have You not delivered this town into my hands? All my life a soldier I've made You prayers and made them straight, I've reared my one true axe against the timber and I've launched it true. My regiment was my duty, and I called Death honest, killing by the book—but it all got scrawled and mucked about and I could not think clear . . . Now I have my duties different. I'm in this town to change all soldiers' duties. My prayer is: Keep my mind clear so that I can weigh Judgement against the Mercy and Judgement against the Blood, and make this Dance as terrible as You have put it into my brain. The Word alone is terrible: the Deed must be worse. But I know it is Your logic and You will provide.

Behind the soldier stands another figure. He is in every way the soldier's opposite. Whereas the soldier's uniform is shining red and spotless, this man's rough black clothes are thick with grime. And his shape offers a contrast. When, like the soldier, he stands to attention, his body is comic and crooked, a question mark set against the straight backbone of the soldier. He imitates the soldier in everything he does. When the soldier crosses his hands to pray, this man does the same. Only in all the man's gestures there is an element of exaggeration: he takes the soldier's meaningful actions and pushes them to absurdity. When the soldier's prayer ends, the man whips

"Arden's Stagecraft" by Albert Hunt. From *Encore,* XII, No. 5 (1965), 9-12.

off his cap. The soldier turns on his heel and leaves without seeing the man. The man remains on the stage, looking up to heaven and smirking. He murmurs, "Amen."

How are we to interpret a scene like this? There are three main possibilities.

(1) The soldier is the hero. He has all the characteristics of a hero. He is tall, handsome, eloquent and he has a good voice. Moreover, his message is clearly true. He has been shocked by a bloody incident in a colonial war and this has convinced him that war is evil. As good liberals we all know, like the soldier, that war is wicked: we are on his side. Emotionally, we identify ourselves totally with the soldier, Serjeant Musgrave. We hardly notice the crooked little figure standing behind him. If we do, he is merely an obscenity, one of the evils against which, with Musgrave, we are ready to fight.

(2) The crooked man—the bargee—is the hero. He is the little man doing down authority. Like Chaplin. Cocking a snook at pomposity. Like Harpo Marx. We identify ourselves totally with the little man. We laugh *with* him through his antics. The soldier becomes completely ridiculous.

(3) We don't identify ourselves totally with either figure. We watch, as we would watch two jugglers in a variety show. And we listen. The soldier is tall, heroic. He is clearly to be admired. But wait. Isn't there something just a bit ridiculous about the soldier's stance? When you see the crooked absurdity of the bargee standing to attention, doesn't the soldier's pose begin to look absurd, too? How ridiculous to stand with your hands clasped like that, talking to nobody!

And yet, there's something noble about the soldier. Set against him the bargee looks like a cheap clown. And the soldier's message is so obviously right—"to change all soldiers' duties."

But wait again. Isn't there something also a bit exaggerated in the soldier's language? What is all this about the Mercy and the Judgement and the Blood and the Word? As the soldier utters the words, he strains towards heaven, as if trying to catch God's ear. The bargee's gestures in imitation invite you to become aware of the soldier's self-dramatisation. Yet the soldier's sense of purpose remains admirable and there's still the element of truth in his message.

Arden presents us with two opposites which illumine each other. The opposites exist in a physical relationship on the stage. If you identify yourself with either—if, for example, the actor playing Musgrave pulls out all the emotional stops and carries you away; or if he exaggerates Musgrave's gestures to the point of caricature—the moral balance of the scene is destroyed.

The first two responses belong to what is still the accepted form of "serious" theatre—the theatre of illusion. The third belongs to a completely different tradition, in which John Arden's work belongs.

II

The naturalist theatre, the theatre of illusion. Everything subordinated to what Samuel Johnson once called "the supposed necessity of making the drama credible." Conversation, gestures, costumes, set, lighting, acting—all aimed at persuading the spectators temporarily to accept that what they are seeing is really happening. Naturalist theatre has, of course, been under attack for a long time. Every critic who's read Gorden Craig knows it's out. The cluttered scenery has been cleared out of Shakespeare, and even the Norfolk cottage in *Roots* (a naturalist play if ever there was one—its strength lies in its naturalist qualities) has been reduced to a skeleton.

But the central assumptions of naturalist theatre—illusion and identification—have scarcely been challenged. We pay lip-service to Brecht—but Martin Esslin can still see Mother Courage as a heroic figure.

The central truth about any theatre that aims at illusion is that it can only succeed to the extent that the spectator's awareness of *what is actually happening* can be broken down. (Which is why, of course, Brecht tells us beforehand what the events shown in a scene will be, so that we can concentrate entirely on *how* they are shown and *why*.) The spectator, of course, never fully accepts what he's seeing as real. But if the illusion is successful, the spectator will be persuaded to blot out that half of his mind that tells him he is only seeing a play.

The simplest way of persuading the spectator to share in the illusion is to draw him *inside* the action by inviting him to become totally identified with one character. You see the world through the eyes of Jimmy Porter or Beattie Bryant. So that when, at the end of *Roots,* Beattie tells you she's talking, you're carried away by her own excitement. You're moved by her joy. You never notice that what she is saying is much the same as what she's been saying all through the play when she's been quoting Ronnie.

But if you identify yourself totally with Musgrave, the play becomes confused.

III

Our "serious" theatre is still judged almost entirely in terms of illusion—see almost any current reviews of Brecht, Arden, or Shakespeare: Olivier's Othello.

But we still have, live, if watered-down, another theatre tradition. Read Arden's description of a pantomime in Dublin where "an individual dressed as a gorilla bounded on to the stage and did a lot of knockabout with two comedians, and then came leaping off into the audience in a completely hideous stage gorilla costume, and raced about the audience, plonked himself down into a fat woman's lap and took her hat off, deposited her hat on a bald man, then flung its arms round another bald man and nuzzled him in the face . . . And just as you began to wonder how far it was going to go, the gorilla suddenly bounded back on to the stage, unzipped the costume and it was an attractive chorus girl in a little dress."

In the "serious" theatre you would be saying, "But how unconvincing! What pretty girl would want to make herself ugly like that? What does this reveal to me about her character?" In pantomime, the scene's success depends on your being constantly aware that what you are seeing is not real. What you enjoy is the knowledge that there's an actor zipped up inside the gorilla. The gorilla impinges on the real world. The hats it takes off and the embarrassment it causes are real. (There's a similar sort of pleasure at a circus, where you know the girl on the tightrope is only pretending that it's difficult—but you also know that if she falls off the pain will be real.)

The final satisfaction of the gorilla comes when you're presented with a surprising physical discovery. The suit is unzipped, and instead of the actor you knew was there, out steps a pretty girl. You are delighted because you've been fooled.

In pantomime you respond directly to a physical happening on the stage.

It's in this popular tradition that Arden's plays belong. Played naturalistically, for illusion, *Live Like Pigs* is crude, and the ballads get in the way, as they did at the Court. Because *Live Like Pigs* is based on music hall. The lines demand to be played out at the audience. The play consists of a series of sketches, woven into a meaningful pattern, and the violence of the clash between gypsies and neighbours is summed up in a music hall gag. "I tear them all up, don't I?" Confronted by disaster, the Sawneys, with anarchic defiance, scatter shreds of washing all over the stage.

Played for identification with the audience, *Musgrave* becomes incomprehensible. For the true statement of the play lies in the way Musgrave's pacifist message is judged against the action of the play and found inadequate. If you're too close to Musgrave, this judgement is never seen.

Played for illusion, *The Happy Haven* is a feeble joke. But *The Happy Haven* descends from a long tradition of commedia del' arte. Arden uses the masks to *call attention* to the fact that we're not seeing real old people—only actors who are showing us what it's like to be old, and who are therefore able to *comment* on old age. (Copperthwaite, in the same play, is a comic version of Musgrave: he has one single purpose, to discover the Elixir of life. He discovers it *accidentally* and is turned into a child—an example of the way Arden uses a popular convention, the child's mask, to explore a complex theme like the limitations of rational thought.)

In all his plays, Arden turns to this popular tradition, not because he wants to "experiment"—we see the results of this kind of experiment in the confusion of the *Marat/Sade,* where, in spite of the pretence that we're seeing a play put on by lunatics, one of the main characters, Marat, remains obstinately a figure of illusion—but because the *meaning* of his plays is expressed in the kind of duality that tradition implies.

To discuss the problem of staging Arden, therefore, is not simply to talk about the problems of technique. Or rather, it's by discussing problems of technique that one begins to come to terms with what Arden has to say.

And what Arden has to say is, I believe, extremely relevant to the central concerns of our time.

Arden's Unsteady Ground

by Richard Gilman

"An object of art is artistic only insofar as it is not real," Ortega y Gasset once wrote, and meant something much broader than an attack upon naturalism. Until we are able to think of drama, for all its physical contingencies and aesthetic impurities, as existing in a different realm from the "real"—the way we are mostly able to think of poetry, painting, music—we will go on disputing over everything that is peripheral and secondary in the work of a playwright like Arden, in the effort to establish its "validity," unconscious that this validity has already been established by the play's own internal processes and conquests.

There is something dispiriting about Arden's own vacillations between apology and peevish resentment. The prefaces to his plays are full of protests against his critics, but also of weakly enunciated and what can only be called supererogatory statements of his dramatic intentions. It is rather painful to hear a playwright of his stature say, as he does in the preface to *Left-Handed Liberty,* that "I am not normally an enthusiast for didactic drama" and then proceed to explicate the play's meaning, as though we had no means of discovering it for ourselves within the work. Arden has some justification insofar as a great many critics—professional and lay—do seem to have been unable to find it, just as they were stumped by the theme of *Serjeant Musgrave's Dance* or of *Live Like Pigs.* Still, however obtuse the response to the latter play was, it needn't have led Arden to such timid, ingenuous, and wholly unnecessary comments as those he made in the preface to the published text:

"Arden's Unsteady Ground" by Richard Gilman. From *Tulane Drama Review,* XI, No. 2 (1966), 54-62.

> When I wrote this play I intended it to be not so much a social document as a study of differing ways of life brought sharply into conflict and both losing their particular virtues under the stress of intolerance and misunderstanding. In other words, I was more concerned with the "poetic" than the "journalistic" structure of the play.

The temptation is to reply, Oh, in the manner of a *New Yorker* newsbreak. The point is that Arden, like Brecht, is much more of an artist than his *obiter dicta* might suggest. Of course, one feels like saying to him, you're not really a didactic playwright, of course you're more interested in poetry than journalism. At the back of these strange tergiversations and pained, naïve avowals one senses a strand of the theatrical climate in England, a weather which is also beginning to take shape here: the need to be concerned (or to appear to be) in one way or another with socially and politically significant material, the fear of being seduced into too thoroughgoing an aesthetic stance, the embarrassment at not having, or not seeming to want to have, a clearly defined social commitment.

To describe oneself as a political or sociological playwright may very well be in this climate a ticket of admission, a way to get in out of the rain. That is to say, it seems clear from the context of Arden's remark, its surrounding clichés about man's being a social and political animal, etc., and first and foremost from the evidence of his plays, that caught between his *predilection d'artist* and his communal sensibilities he covers himself (without guile or hope of concrete gain, it goes without saying) by pleading both. To the ideologues who would enlist his dramas in support of programs and are baffled by their resistance, he speaks wanly of poetic structure taking precedence over journalistic; to the formalists who might wish him to be less reportorial than he is, he points to the necessary basis in concrete events which all his plays exhibit.

Yet it should be obvious that the "events" of these plays are not simply dramatizations or, more subtly, aestheticized analogues of those other, historical happenings, and that the poetic interest he takes in them is not simply greater than his interest in reportage but of a different kind altogether. That Arden is in some sense a thoroughly political playwright has never been at issue; every one of his works is steeped in politics and is the product of an imagination for which non-political reality—private myth, insular fortune, the discrete ego—would seem to have no independent standing as material for drama. No, what is at issue is the fate of political subject matter in his plays, the unpolitical uses to which he puts it, the transformations it undergoes under the action of his half-lyrical, half-civic and polemical sensibility, the sensibility, one might call it, of a passionate citizen, a brooding burgher.

What is the nature of political reality and how does the rest of the life of man (the title of his first play, a radio script) relate to it, or rather how does man's life come to know in the crucible of power, rule, and social governance? What are the prices that political necessity exacts from the moral self and the psyche? How does one celebrate life in the midst of abstractions? Such are the chief energizing questions of Arden's plays. They are what make him something extraordinarily different from a traditionally "political" or "sociological" playwright, by which, if definitions and terminology have not already descended into chaos, we mean someone for whom the immediate data of political or social organization are paramount, for whom, too, the choices involved in public existence are more or less co-terminous with the choices involved in all existence, and for whom, finally, a play is an exemplification, subtle or gross, of the virtue of making the right choices or of the cost of failing to make them.

For Arden, however, there are no clear choices—which is what pitches him above ideology; although there is a clear necessity to act publicly—which is what keeps his plays anchored in a perception of social actuality. Again and again, in one form or another, he questions, or rather raises to the dignity and ambiguous sincerity of a question, something we might call the humanness of politics, its role and function as the process and measure of our life in common. That public life *has* to be organized, and that power *has* to be exerted, are the assumptions, with their roots in a tragic awareness, of all his plays; that the private self rebels against this inexorability, in the name of its spontaneous, wayward life, of all distinct values and of the simplicities of what it considers its natural choices, is the agency which generates the "drama" of his dramas. If there is any modern book outside the literature of the theatre which provides a clue to Arden's temperament and procedures, it is surely Freud's *Civilization and its Discontents.*

This conflict of the self, or its spontaneous element, with the organizing, abstract, equally self-interested and therefore inherently repressive action of politics is complemented and enlarged by another encounter which runs through most of Arden's work. This is the confrontation of a deadly impulse towards purity (which may be found both within the actions of power and in all fanatic attempts to do away with it) and the impure, flawed, capricious, and uncodifiable nature of reality beneath our schemes for organizing it.

In *Left-Handed Liberty,* King John replies to Pandulph, the Papal Legate who in his distaste for the imperfections of the palpable has called him a "dandelion": "I am partial to dandelions. Coarse in texture, I know, and the scent is undistinguished and they are far too prolific. But powdered across the slope of a green meadow, all those thousand dots of gold—who could want to be rid of them?" The King then goes on to explain why the Charter he has signed is protected against becoming the repressive instrument such abstract documents are likely to turn into: "I said: make those clauses general—lax, if you like—because by their very laxness they go some way to admit the existence of dandelions, of disobedient women, and ribbons of cloth-of-gold."

Earlier in the play Pandulph has sung of the mental tyrant's dream of absolute order and purity in the organization of existence and of attitudes towards it:

> Storm breaks in among the perfect circles,
> Every day a puff of wind or a rumble of thunder
> Declares some vain attempt to declare—what?
> Very busy very busy very busy!
> Whatever it is, it will be vain,
> It will be some broken blunder:
> But we who preserve the circles
> Preserve their unfaulted music . . .

To which John, accounting for his backing and filling, his devious behavior and slippery dealings, replies: "I am delivering the antidote to all those circles with no kinks in . . ."

The pure, that which refuses to admit the exceptional, the capricious, or the contradictory, and the abstract, that which incarcerates living phenomena in reductive systems, are the enemies of the actual, and it is this enmity which, under a variety of grave and comic masks, is on exhibit throughout Arden's theatre. On one level the abstractive impulse allied with power results in men being treated as things. At its most burlesque—and most schematic—this is a chief theme of *The Happy Haven.* Here a group of people in a home for the aged are made the object of a scientific—more properly, alchemical—experiment on the part of their doctor, who has developed a formula for making them young again. That they turn the tables on him in the end, forcing him to drink his own potion and thus return to helpless infancy, is the play's farcical mainspring but not its best imaginative possibility.

If anything, this comic revenge motif obscures something much more interesting and original. For what the inmates are really trying to hold on to is their integrity, which consists—against the pretense of the state and the tastes of everyone—precisely in being old, being what they are. There can be few rivals in recent literature to Arden's intuition of what old age consists in and feels like than the song of the old woman, Mrs. Phineus, rightly quoted by John Russell Taylor in his essay on Arden as an example of his writing's "hard-won strength and sinew":

> I'm an old old lady
> And I don't have long to live.
> I am only strong enough to take
> Not to give. No time left to give.
> I want to drink, I want to eat,
> I want my shoes taken off my feet.
> I want to talk but not to walk
> Because if I walk, I have to know
> Where it is I want to go.
> I want to sleep but not to dream
> I want to play and win every game
> To live with love but not to love
> The world to move but me not move
> I want I want for ever and ever.
> The world to work, the world to be clever.
> Leave me be, but don't leave me alone.
> That's what I want. I'm a big round stone
> Sitting in the middle of a thunderstorm.

Yet they are all seduced at first, as anyone would be, by the possibility of rejuvenation, until through a "game of truth" which they play they come to see that life is irreversible, that nothing would be changed by the doctor's elixir:

> *Hardrader.* I hope I would find a healthy humane existence.
> *Golightly.* No no, excuse me, no, Mr. Hardrader. You would be as lonely as ever you were. I know, because I would be, too. Isn't it terrifying?

The implication in the patients' discovery is that while power, in this case the hunger for far-reaching control of biological existence itself, will pursue its own ends, the proper resistance to it is sometimes not counter-power but the sustaining authority of the truth. When the patients get back at the doctor they accomplish an act in the realm of power, a reversal which satisfies our primitive sense of social justice, the villain getting his come-uppance; but when they slip out of the reach of power by understanding its limits and miscalculations they truly undermine it—and move the play a long notch up from didactic farce. Too confined, however, to immediate sociological considerations—his target, in addition to the doctor's arrogance and inhuman scientism, is the complacency of the institution's benefactors and trustees, the patients' "betters"—Arden settles in this play for an obvious truth and satisfaction when he had much richer ones within his grasp.

In *Live Like Pigs,* the events are much more realistic but the action is far less programmatic. The play concerns a nomadic, "uncivilized" group of people who run up against both lower-middle class propriety—in the persons of their neighbors in a housing project to which they have been compelled to move from their previous home in an abandoned streetcar—and the leveling, hygienic processes of the welfare state, which cannot tolerate their dirt, their immorality, and, above all, their lack of ambition. Against the impersonal functioning of authority, which does have on its side, however, a clarity of purpose and a basis in reasonableness, their only weapons are an ability to side-step the rules and the heavy formless strength of their refusal to be assimilated. They are besieged by papers, forms, the instruments of civilization but also the artillery of bureaucrats:

Rachel. He says, "Complaints relating to condition of—of aforesaid residence. And gardens appertaining." Ach, all that it is—words.

Rosie. They send those words at us under the door all the time. It's not right. What can *we* do when we get them? They put us, it's like a dog in a box, you can stick spikes through every corner at him and he's no place to turn at all.

To their neighbors, proper, tacky, narrowly ambitious, terrified of them but also fascinated, they are invaders from a world of irrationality and brute appetite, anachronisms in an age of universal plumbing and savings accounts. In time, fear and fascination turn into rage, in a scene which Arden drew from an actual occurrence and which has its historical analogues here in the riots that have broken out in white neighborhoods when a Negro family has moved in. To this collapse of civilized restraints in the face of the unassimilated, Arden's nomads respond with an inchoate roar of blatant perverse animality, a turning of the screw. In an action reminiscent of one in Zola's *Germinal,* where a strapping girl striker thrusts her gigantic nude bottom in the direction of a phalanx of bosses and soldiers and invites their homage to it, Big Rachel, the earthy, whorish "mother" of the clan, assails the besiegers of their house (the attackers are mostly women), her words "interspersed with sheer animal noises":

> You want us out o' here? I tell you, you want more'n you know you want, you darling lovely girls! We'll come out, oh we'll come out, you'll not forget us when we come. I tell you: we live like bloody animals, you don't know what animals are! You hide in your hutches in your good warm straw and you think you got thirty-two teeth in your heads; but we carry fifty-three ohoho-rho—and there's blood for each of 'em between the leg and the neck, when *we* come, when *we* come blooding . . .

But the defiance cannot be sustained. Rachel's bellow has been into the void, into the emptiness that lies between incommensurate existences and contradictory codes. In the end social order, majority values, and the weight of the unexceptionable prevail. As Sailor Sawney, the clan's patriarch, tells Rachel:

> You don't know this bastardy-like of folk like I do . . . Aye, aye, they belong inside their hutches . . . And they don't fight strong. But

> when they're out and calling *you* out, they don't run home soon, neither. They're in their crowd and they'll swarm you and you'll drown. Live and let live, I say. But that's been broke into two by this lot . . . They're feard o' Big Rachel, O.K. Begod they're that feard of her, they'll kill her. All of us. Just cos we live.

They are not killed but they are indeed "drowned," swarmed under, defeated and exiled from any life they might have in the eyes of others. There is no place for them, Arden is saying, in a society which roots out the indigestible and is forever trying to see to it that there are no loose ends. As their members are dispersed all they can do is repeat, like children protesting against rationality and authority, the last two lines of the primitive little religious verse they had earlier sung at the windows as a talismanic act to keep out the mob:

> Window close and window true
> In and out and who comes through?
> Mary and Jesus and the Twelve Tall Riders
> Nobody else nobody else nick nack noo!

Live Like Pigs is a robust play, humorous, touching, scarifying by turns, but it suffers from a central opacity and its dramatic trajectory is impeded. John Russell Taylor has ascribed the puzzled, disgruntled public response to it to Arden's refusal to take sides, to choose between the opposing ways of life represented by the anarchic Sawneys and the law-abiding Jacksons. And it is true that the former are not romanticized; their dirt is real and unpleasant, their moral ugliness is plain to see. Yet Taylor's point is an answer only to those ideologues who wanted Arden to go all the way in his defense of the outsider (or, for certain audiences, the insider), to be explicit about it, to draw conclusions and a moral. He has not done that but he has also failed, despite his clear intentions, to give the Jacksons—his representatives of the socially conventional—anything more than a thin, conventional dramatic reality.

Taylor stresses the fact that the Jacksons are not meant to be representative, that they exist as individuals. Doubtless this was what was intended, but it remains true that they lapse back into the general and representational through their lack of detail, interest, and specificity. Beyond that, there is no real clash except on the level of physical action; the cards may be stacked against the Sawneys socially but dramatically they have all the aces, so that Arden's vision of an inevitable conflict, the world as a place of incompatible entities which nevertheless have equal right to existence, has to be largely extrapolated from the play instead of finding its true and adequate form within it.

Despite the much greater acclaim it has received, *Serjeant Musgrave's Dance* is as widely misunderstood as *Live Like Pigs,* but in this case the play, although suffering from certain structural weaknesses, is perfectly well in possession of its theme and idea. Almost universally described as an "anti-war" drama, *Musgrave* is nevertheless a source of extreme bafflement precisely to those viewers who persist in seeing it that way. Its militant pacifists come to ruin, its denunciation of war seems confined to colonial aggression, it seems to throw up its hands in the face of the problem of violence. Indeed, regarded as a political exhortation, *Musgrave* is extraordinarily ineffective, a lame sermon; but it is not a political play except in the sense that Arden wishes to test certain modes of political action by more rigorous standards than that action can ever provide in itself and in so doing test something more profound than politics.

Musgrave is, once again, a play about purity, except that here the impulse and ravishment of the pure is non-institutional, centered in the figure of a fanatic for whom the world's fire must be fought with fire. For Black Jack Musgrave, the ostensible recruiting sergeant but secret "priest" and avenging prophet, his mission is to strike a blow against violence and the cruelty of power politics, an act—the taking of twenty-five lives for the five his men were responsible for in some unnamed colony (Britain's role in the Cyprus upheaval was Arden's historical datum)—designed to teach the townspeople the horror and futility of political aggression and the exercise of military power. It is "God's dance on this earth" that he will perform, and in these words—so like Pandulph's in *Left-Handed Liberty*—the fierce, inflexible, proprietary nature of his sense of power are revealed.

What is most crucial to an understanding of the play is to center one's attention on the manner in which Musgrave shoulders aside all phenomena that may impede his straight true course to his murderously righteous objective. To the barmaid who threatens the irruption of love and desire onto the clean lines of his scheme and its philosophical framework he sets forth his "higher" values:

> Look, lassie, anarchy: now, we're soldiers. Our work isn't easy, no and it's not soft: it's got a strong name—duty. And it's drawn out straight and black for us, a clear plan. But if you come to us with what you call your life and love—*I'd* call it your indulgence—and you scribble all over that plan, and make it crooked, dirty, idle, untidy, *bad*—there's anarchy.

Much later, after his plan is revealed and has disastrously failed and he himself is awaiting death, he is still unable to comprehend where he went wrong:

> *Musgrave*. Good order and the discipline: it's the only road I know. Why can't you see it?
>
> *Mrs. Hitchcock*. All I can see is Crooked Joe Bludgeon having his dance out in the middle of fifty Dragoons! It's time you learnt your life, you big proud serjeant. Listen: last evening you told all about this anarchy and where it came from—like, scribble all over with life or love, and that makes anarchy. Right?
>
> *Musgrave*. Go on.
>
> *Mrs. Hitchcock*. Then *use* your Logic—if you can. Look at it this road: here we are, and we'd got life and love. Then *you* came in and you did your scribbling where nobody asked you. Aye, it's arsey-versey to what you said, but it's still an anarchy, isn't it? And it's all your work.
>
> *Musgrave*. Don't tell me there was life or love in this town.
>
> *Mrs. Hitchcock*. There was. There was hungry men, too—fighting for their food. But *you* brought in a different war.
>
> *Musgrave*. I brought it in to end it.
>
> *Attercliffe*. To end it by its own rules: no bloody good. She's right, you're wrong.

On the simplest level Musgrave's crime is that of practicing homeopathic medicine: he would put a stop to killing by killing, the end justifying the means. But more profoundly the play brings into question the nature of all abstract values, when they become embodied in a passionate urgency toward social reformation. The horror such zeal can bring lies in its obliviousness of complexity, the way it cuts down the living in its pursuit of what is seen to bring death, the way its insistence on purity becomes a fulfillment not of human desires or needs but of its own internal propositions. That *Serjeant Musgrave's Dance* leaves the problem of political violence where it found it, offering no prescriptions and no programs, is exactly why it is not a "political" play; it is not real, it is an artifact of the dramatic imagination, and it leaves the problem of violence to those agencies, outside art, whose province it properly is.

If *Musgrave* is a play about the consequences of purity, *Armstrong's Last Goodnight* is one about impurity, about the brindled color of politics and the devastations brought about by the perennial conflict between the general and the particular in society, the rival claims of authority and the individual. The clash between Johnny Armstrong of Gilnockie, a provincial lord and freebooter, and King James of Scotland, who is struggling to establish a centralized, secure realm, is, the play makes clear, an inevitable one. There is no thorough-going villain and no unassailable hero; "here," Sir David Lindsay, the "very subtle practiser" who is the King's diplomatic troubleshooter, announces at the end, "may ye read the varieties of dishonour."

It is clear that Arden's sympathies lie with Armstrong. For Armstrong contains in himself an element of passionate life, a simplicity and directness which seen from a certain point of view puts the deviousness and calculated operations of the state to shame. His virtues, however, are what constitute him as the very principle of anarchic individualism, which brings him into inevitable collision with the generalizing principle of the state. The latter must seek his betrayal and death for its own physical self-protection, but even more for the preservation of its existential nature—authority cannot be another thing than that which strikes down whatever attempts to thrust itself before the general welfare.

Yet nothing is clearer than that the action of authority in bringing about Armstrong's death has only a provisional value, a temporary effectiveness, and that in the moral realm, whose values are different, judgment will continue to be pronounced upon it. As Lindsay tells the king, summing up the affair:

> The man is deid, there will be nae war with England: this year. There will be small turbulence on the border: this year. And what we have done is no likely to be forgotten: this year, the neist year, and mony a year after that.

Still, we are witnessing the *varieties* of dishonor. Armstrong has been no blameless victim; in his arrogance and unbridled egotism he has treacherously killed a rival laird, and has demonstrated a childish, overweening concern for the appurtenances of power, with no sense of responsibility to go with it. It is one of the deepest proofs of Arden's artistry that virtue is not allowed to accumulate in Armstrong's hands, just as it is not allowed to accumulate in the hands of any of his erstwhile heroes, those passionate, anarchic souls who struggle inconclusively against the realities of the structure of the world.

It is Lindsay, the keen diplomat, who understands those realities best. Yet his skepticism and sophisticated mastery of *realpolitik* are not permitted to have the final word. For his consciousness and rationality, his wit and sense of the way the world runs, are not ultimately serious; simulacra of seriousness, they are actually the instruments of a game he plays, the game played by anyone who is too civilized, too given over, that is to say, to one side—practical, abstract, logical—of the perennial conflict that runs through man's organized life in common. Like Musgrave's instruction in the realities of his own life by Mrs. Hitchcock, Lindsay hears his truth from his secretary, McGlass:

> Ye did tak pride in your recognition of the fallibility of man. Recognize your aim, then, Lindsay; ye have ane certain weakness, ye can never accept the gravity of ane other man's violence. For you yourself hae never been grave in the hale of your life . . . your rationality and practicality has broke itself to pieces, because ye wad never muster the needful gravity to gar it stand as strang, as Gilnockie's fury.

Gilnockie's fury stands on the other side, with its own consequences in undiscipline, imbalance, and self-injury, but real, distinct, to be accounted for. On that side, too, stands his sexual passion, in Arden's work a principal agency of opposition to the rationalizing of human activity. The Lady's Song, invoking that passion and summoning it forth, is one of Arden's most splendid lyrics:

> When I stand in the full direction of your force
> Ye need nae wife nor carl to stand
> Alsweel beside ye and interpret.
> There is in me ane knowledge, potent, secret

That I can set to rin ane sure concourse
Of bodily and ghaistly strength betwixt the blood
Of me and of the starkest man alive. My speed
Hangs twin with yours: and starts are double flood:
Will you with me initiate the deed
And saturait consequence thereof—
Crack aff with your great club
The barrel-hoops of love
And let it pour
Like the enchantit quern that boils red-herring broo
Until it gars upswim the goodman's table and his door
While all his house and yard and street
Swill reeken, greasy, het, oer-drownit sa-foot four.

With its range and sure-handed balancing of contrarieties, its supple, muscular rhetoric (the sixteenth century Scots dialect is much easier to understand in performance than has been made out) and its fusion of lyric energy and reflective strength, *Armstrong's Last Goodnight* may well be the masterpiece among Arden's non-masterpieces. In any case, it most fully exhibits his new species of post-political and post-ideological drama, resisting partisanship, disclaiming solutions, neither hortatory nor tendentious yet strenuously involved in actuality.

Probably the most frequent comment that has been made about Arden is that he is unclassifiable, that he cannot be put into a category. The argument is sound up to a point, but beyond that it gets specious and is an evasion. No true artist is classifiable, if by classification we mean a reductive, imprisoning act which deprives his work of the right to conjure up unheard-of entities. But it does no service to Arden to treat his plays as though no controlling impulse and thematic concern were to be discovered in them, as though they were a series of discrete, arbitrary phenomena. What he has done, an important act for the theatre, is boundable and can be identified: it is to have taken the social and political life of man and rescued it, as a subject for drama, from didacticism on the one hand and from impressionism on the other. The new ground he occupies could scarcely be expected to be steady.

The Ascension of John Osborne

by Charles Marowitz

If one looks closely at the crotchety, constipated, hypercritical figure of Martin Luther in John Osborne's newest play, one is forcibly reminded of that fuming British malcontent, Jimmy Porter; a protestant who bitched against the Welfare State as vehemently as the theologian wrangled with the Pope. The similarities do not end there.

Despite the jump in time, the clerical context and the change of venue, the play is not (as has been charged here) a *departure* for Osborne. There is a clear link-up between Luther's sixteenth-century Germany and our time. In both, the sense of cosmic imminence is very strong. "The Last Judgement isn't to come. It's here and now," says Luther, and the doomsday-mountain-squatters and the nuclear-psychotics echo his words. The church-sale of indulgences is put forward as if it were a commercial advertisement, and the suggestion here is that the Catholic Church at its lowest moral ebb is an appropriate symbol for modern ad-mass culture. And who is the cleric Tetzel but a kind of bloated Arthur Godfrey pushing piety with the same unctuousness used to boost Lipton's Tea?

The Osborne of *Look Back in Anger* and *The Entertainer* gave us the *temperature* of social protest. And it was blisteringly hot. In *The World of Paul Slickey,* no longer content with the charged implication and the social inference, Osborne issued indictments. One of these was made out for the church. There was something compulsive in the way that Osborne humiliated his churchmen in

"The Ascension of John Osborne" by Charles Marowitz. From *Tulane Drama Review* VII, No. 2 (1962), 175-79.

Slickey. I have a stark image of an obscenely capering clergyman shedding all the moral restraints one usually associates with the cloth. Osborne seemed to be taking it out on the church because of some fundamental failing, and it was tinged with a personal bitterness—as if Osborne himself had been let down.

The religious disturbance is implicit in all the earlier plays. In his first play, *Epitaph for George Dillon,* there is an arbitrary scene whose only purpose is to deflate the condescending, sold-on-God visitor to the Elliot home. And if we ask ourselves (as so many have) what was bugging Jimmy Porter and George Dillon, the answer would seem to be: loss of faith. Jimmy's plea for "a little ordinary enthusiasm" and Archie Rice's reverence for that "pure, just natural noise" emanating from "an old fat negress getting up to sing about Jesus or something like that" both suggest a yearning for spiritual elevation. The passion that Jimmy Porter cannot muster because "there aren't any good, brave causes left" is the very protoplasm of faith.

It is almost as if Osborne, tracing skepticism down to its roots, had to move from George Dillon to Jimmy Porter to Archie Rice to Martin Luther—almost is if they were all part of the same family. Porter was the overt cynic Dillon was fast becoming, and Archie Rice the exhausted version of both. The springs of that doubt and disillusion can be seen to issue from a sixteenth-century fountainhead. It was Martin Luther who institutionalized doubt. His Rome was the most impregnable of all Establishments—its holy orders an array of Yes Men that makes the Madison Avenue hirelings sound like rampaging individualists. Luther's won't-take-cant-for-an-answer intellect produced the revolution that Jimmy Porter could only imagine. Both threw bricks at stained-glass windows, but whereas Jimmy ran away, Luther moved in and set up shop.

Structurally, Osborne's new play is a series of taut interviews interspersed with sermons and smeared thick with cathedral atmosphere. Formalistically, Osborne (like practically every other modern playwright) appears to be under the sway of Bertolt Brecht. Like Brecht, he has strung together a series of short, stark tableaux. Like Brecht, he has backed them with evocative hangings (flags, banners, tapestries, crucifixes). Like Brecht, he employs a narrator to fill in background and make comment. Like Brecht, he has balanced the man and the social structure so that every moment of one produces a gesture from the other. But unlike Brecht, he has not endowed his play with that added intellectual dimension around which the drama may cohere. He has not, in this tart dramatization of history, furnished an underlying concept with which to interpret events.

Spectacle and rhetoric propel the play's first two acts, but by Act Three it comes to a dead stop because language which has already posited the argument, no longer has a job to perform. The only promising dramatic situation in the play concerns Luther's encouragement and subsequent betrayal of the peasants in their revolt against the lords. This is merely reported after the event in a beautifully written narrative speech which doesn't make up for the lack of action. This is the Brechtian influence at its most destructive. The dramatic climaxes are siphoned dry; characters are involved with the intellectual implications of their behavior rather than with the blood and bone of their situations. A narrative, imagistic language is giving us the "point" of the Luther story in a series of historical passages annotated with theological footnotes. The strongest character in the second half is a Knight who helped put down the peasants' rebellion, and what gives him such presence is the fact that he has just waged war and arrives at least with the residue of an involvement. The real battle has been in Luther's conscience and we have felt only its mildest repercussions. No one has come forward to oppose our protagonist. His anti-clerical father has raged only against losing a son to the monastery. The Pope has threatened but backed down. The beaten peasants have shied off with their tails between their legs. From scene to scene we find ourselves being cheated by authenticity.

The play's final moments emphasize the dearth of development. Luther's second dialogue with Staupitz points up how little we know about either character. The friendly old churchman remains nothing more than a theological straight-man leading Luther into aphorisms and reflection. The worst-written scene in the play shows us Luther, the family man, bussing his baby and being lovingly henpecked by a thoroughly characterless wife. In place of the last-act solidification of ideas (not a desirable way to write a play, but obviously the kind of play Osborne *was* writing), we get the scene of pregnant ambiguity which invites us to moor the play in whichever dock we like, as the writer wasn't going anywhere in particular anyway.

After the tapestries and crucifixes have been struck, and the ring of the language died away, we ask ourselves what is the lesson of *Luther*. Behind peppery images like "empty as a nun's womb" and "the world's straining anus," we try to discern the mind of the twentieth-century playwright.

To judge by the play's final sentiments, it would seem that God is in His heaven and sometimes out of town, and if we are all patient and courageous, He may return in our lifetime. But no, surely John Osborne hasn't fashioned all this to project such a double-barreled homily. If we interpret the play's undercurrent, it is that personal faith rather than institutional dogma (commitment?) is the way to salvation. (Or if not salvation, at least to security and influence, for in his later days Luther was a much respected hellfireist who, after granting clergy permission to marry, took an ex-nun to his own cloister-bed and fathered five little Lutherans.) But all of this remains extra-theatrical speculation and no theory, no matter how valid, seems to make that necessary circuit which links the mind of the playwright to the imagination of the audience.

If the play proves nothing about Luther it proves a great deal about John Osborne. It proves that he has the ability to grasp dramatic ideas and the language to convey them on a hard, bright poetical level. Also, he can don period costumes and still hold a twentieth century stance, and in a theatre where an historical milieu automatically produces turgid posturing, this is a real asset. His structural and intellectual shortcomings do not diminish these gifts.

Osborne, I would guess, is fishing round for a new theme—or rather a new objective correlative in which to express his old theme: personal idealism in collision with institutional dogmas. He has gravitated from anger to contemplation, and that is a healthy progress. One looks forward to his next work with exactly the same eagerness that preceded *Luther*—that preceded *Slickey*—that seems to precede everything the man writes.

At the start of what promises to be the swinging sixties, Osborne remains the most ornery dramatist in England. He still smarts, seethes and occasionally rages. He refuses to conform to other people's idea of his nonconformity. He rejects the cosy club chair and the gutless protest that crackles in the lounge and smolders on the street. He still winces at the stench in his country and refuses to pretend it is only someone burning leaves in the back yard.

He is the closest thing England has to a Norman Mailer. Like the terror of Greenwich Village, he is at war with "the shits" and will not give them any quarter. He too uses the daily newspaper as a sounding board and recently published a hate-letter to England which only a Jonathan Swift could have duplicated. When he is harassed by petty columnists, he slaps them with law suits, and has probably been involved in more litigation than William Schwenk Gilbert. He produces in me a warm sense of security, for I always feel that he is one of the few (small "c") committed playwrights who really writes out of a conviction—that it is a social and humanist conviction and not an allegiance to maintain the fashion of the irate, verbose radical—and that unlike the (capital "C") Committed writers, he is not partial to anything except his art.

Dialogue in Pinter and Others

by John Russell Brown

Harold Pinter has been writing long enough for the shape of his plays, their mechanism, to be easily recognised: a small group of characters in a complex situation; at first both characters and situation are presented obscurely but through a number of surprises or shocks—often contrived with an obvious ingenuity—the audience is led to a clearer and deeper knowledge of the characters. The action of his plays can almost be represented by a formula so that every revue can now have its pinter-play and at small art theatres sub-pinters flourish.

The plays are, formally, old-fashioned character plays, or small parts of them. The dramatist has talked about writing *The Caretaker:*

> At the end of *The Caretaker,* there are two people alone in a room, and one of them must go in such a way as to produce a sense of complete separation and finality. I thought originally that the play must end with the violent death of one at the hands of the other. But then I realised, when I got to the point, that the characters as they had grown could never act in this way. Characters always grow out of all proportion to your original conception of them, and if they don't the play is a bad one. (*New Theatre Magazine,* II (1961), 10)

The new playwright is then the portrayer of character, new in the shortness of his plays, their small casts and the replacement of conventional plot development by strange and often menacing events. His plays are half character studies and half fantasy or imitation of parts of an early Hitchcock film.

"Dialogue in Pinter and Others" by John Russell Brown. From *The Critical Quarterly,* VII, No. 3 (1965), 225-43.

Yet still Pinter remains inimitable; his individual quality is now clearly recognised. At first he was confused with N. F. Simpson, possibly because *The Hole* by Simpson and *The Room* by Pinter are both organised around the clarification of situation. But the differences are in substance rather than form—to make, momentarily, this difficult distinction. The composition of the clay is more important than the shaping of the pot. Of course the two processes cannot be divided, and in both Pinter has been to some extent original; but it is the substance of his plays, their moment to moment life as sustained by dialogue, that remains Pinter's own and repays closest attention. Journalists have called it "brilliant," "individual," "exciting," "poetic."

As an example, here are two men having breakfast together, taken from *The Collection:*

Bill. What time did you get in?
Harry. Four.
Bill. Good party?
Pause.
Harry. You didn't make any toast this morning.
Bill. No. Do you want some?
Harry. No. I don't.
Bill. I can if you like.
Harry. It's all right. Don't bother.
Pause.
How are you spending your day today?
Bill. Go and see a film, I think.
Harry. Wonderful life you lead. (*Pause.*) Do you know some maniac telephoned you last night?
Bill looks at him.
Just as I got in. Four o'clock. Walked in the door and the telephone was ringing.
Bill. Who was it?
Harry. I've no idea.
Bill. What did he want?
Harry. You. He was shy, wouldn't tell me his name.
Bill. Huh.
Pause.
Harry. Who could it have been?
Bill. I've no idea . . .

This is remarkable dialogue. Obviously banal, it must be scrutinized in order to see the ways in which it works, and how well it works.

Such an analysis will also show Pinter's originality working towards the same kind of effects in dialogue as the innovations of other writers and thinkers of the present time. Pinter himself has said that he is not conscious of any particular influence on his writing, other than Samuel Beckett; and he added that if this is discernible it is due to his general admiration for the "texture" of his dialogue rather than any allusive intention (*Op. Cit.*, p. 9). Pinter's affinities to other writers do not demonstrate precise indebtedness, but the many ways in which his dialogue responds to contemporary attitudes and concerns. For more than fashionable reasons Pinter is intimately and consistently "with it."

The dialogue's triviality first claims attention: parties, toast, films, the telephone. This is not a Wordsworthian "simpleness"; Pinter is not trying to show that unconsidered elements of urban life are really very important. He does not sweep the dust off the little rooms we live in, and make them and the action "fine" or "more meaningful."

Sometimes he uses, like Chekhov, the allusive or representational importance of small details, their "inner truth." Here is a passage from *The Dwarfs* about Mark's new suit:

Mark. It's got a zip at the hips.
Len. A zip at the hips? What for?
Mark. Instead of a buckle. It's neat.
Len. Neat? I should say it's neat.
Mark. No turn-ups.
Len. I can see that. Why didn't you have turn-ups?
Mark. It's smarter without turn-ups.
Len. Of course it's smarter without turn-ups.
Mark. I didn't want it double-breasted.
Len. Double-breasted? Of course you couldn't have it double-breasted.

This is modishly trivial, and yet something like the talk about the green belt on Natasha's pink dress in *The Three Sisters*. Only in Chekhov the effect is more overt. The belt is insisted upon with the wearer's first entrance, and picked up again in the course of the play. In the last Act Natasha criticises Irena's belt: "you want something brighter to go with that dress." And still more significantly this short remark is followed at once with "I'll tell them to put flowers all round here, lots of flowers, so that we get plenty of scent from them . . ." So a trivial detail represents character, giving an example of Natasha's strong tasteless life; and, in its last context, it leads the audience to associate her over-bearing vitality with more general images in their own memory. The belt enables Chekhov to give size, clarity and generality to Natasha. Toozenbach's last speech, delighting in the beautiful fir trees and then noticing a single dead one, makes a similar effect even more inescapably; the allusiveness is spelt out:

> It's all dried-up, but it's still swaying in the wind along with the others. And in the same way, it seems to me that, if I die, I shall still have a share in life somehow or other. . . .

Pinter's use of mundane detail—parties, toast, films, telephone—is also like another element in Chekhov's writing. After Toozenbach's allusion to the fir trees he calls Irena whom he loves and then he has another kind of trivial speech that needs a stage-direction to explain—

> *Toozenbach (not knowing what to say).* I didn't have any coffee this morning. Will you tell them to get some ready for me?

—and so he goes off quickly to his expected death. Here the triviality does not have obvious visual repercussions in the audience's consciousness; at first reading it could seem an anti-climax, less poetical, less directly meaningful. But its effect is indirect: the very triviality, in contrast with the more "philosophical" preceding speech, shows the power of Toozenbach's embarrassment and his concern for Irena. Saying the first thing that comes into his mind expresses more than any considered speech might do: his desires, his instinctive concerns. In performance an actor can here suggest the character's longing for a regular, shared life; his desire for Irena's help and co-operation; his own forgetfulness; his knowledge of his own forgetfulness; his desire to protect Irena from a knowledge of his danger. None of this can be said directly in words, for much may be subconscious in Toozenbach at this moment and the situation is not suitable for a declaration. Moreover this character is afraid of expressing himself fully. For an actor the speech is a huge opportunity for expressing a newly developed involvement; he will use the apparent change of subject, the generality and then direct address, the uncertainty indicated in the stage-direction, his physical posture, broken rhythm, manner of moving off-stage.

In stage dialogue triviality can thus impress character intimately and subtly and can express unconscious reactions, especially in situations which obviously call for words of greater import. Pinter uses trivia in this way consistently, and is here in line with many more writers and thinkers of the present century. Freud in *The Psychopathology of Everyday Life* (1901) has described such phenomena with neat documentation, and has sometimes quoted much earlier authority. He used Laurence Sterne to speak for the importance of trivial gestures:

> I am not at all surprized that *Gregory* of *Nazianzum,* upon observing the hasty and untoward gestures of *Julian,* should foretell he would one day become an apostate;—or that *St. Ambrose* should turn his *Amanuensis* out of doors, because of an indecent motion of his head, which went backwards and forwards like a flail; . . . . . . There are a thousand unnoticed openings, continued my father, which let a penetrating eye at once into a man's soul; and I maintain it, added he, that a man of sense does not lay down his hat in coming into a room,—or take it up in going out of it, but something escapes, which discovers him.

Through the usually "unnoticed" details of speech, Pinter, like some others at all times and like many writing today, can "let a penetrating eye at once into a man's soul." He has outgone his predecessors most obviously in the ways in which he has seized on the audience's penetration. His dramas cannot be received without a continuous intimation of the unconscious lives of his characters.

Pinter's most obvious devices for invoking the right attention for his plays are menace and muddle. Particularly in his earliest plays, he contrives the action with Hitchcock alertness. He relies on the unexpected call or the sudden descent of a previously unidentified lift in *The Dumb-Waiter*. Stanley, in *The Birthday Party,* tells Meg a story of men coming with a van containing a wheelbarrow and knocking on her door and then, immediately, Lulu knocks on the door. In the later plays Pinter is more discreet in the use of external stimuli to attention, as in the single occasion when the milkman breaks into the closed world of *The Lover*. But his use of muddle, or confused and confusing exposition, continues into his latest plays. The audience does not know what characters are called or what has happened: whether Goldberg is Nat or Simey, whether the visitor is called Davies, Jenkins or Mac Davies, whether the wife recognises the husband, or what if anything was done in a hotel in Leeds. Sometimes the repeated facts about people and places are clearly contradictory. At other times the places and names are left vague: who is Monty—if he is anybody—to whom Stanley is taken at the end of *The Birthday Party*? Or doubt is thrown on an apparently simple fact by confusion in related facts: are Davies' papers at Sidcup?—his case was not at the cafe. The audience is puzzled and *therefore* wishes to notice.

But both these devices operate under the law of diminishing returns; as if he were crying wolf, Pinter runs the risk that the audience, expecting to be puzzled, ceases to be truly puzzled; still more, that the expectant audience ceases to be menaced. Other devices for ensuring that trivia do the necessary work for the dramatist are less obvious in their operation. In the first place we should not underestimate the effect of Pinter's unusual insistence and consistency: there is no escape for the audience in roundly phrased statements of meaning, or in regular explanations, investigations, trials, confessions, self-revealing and irrevocable letters or diaries, or any of the familiar expository aids of the realistic or poetic dramatist.

Pinter's musical sense, which gives to his dialogue a light suppleness, is also an important factor in keeping the audience's subtle attention. By varying rhythms and by repetitions he can give to Mick's speech about bus routes a growing forcefulness to which the audience can hardly fail to respond. In a conversation that is apparently concerned solely with minor details in the finishing of a gentleman's suit, he suggests the hesitations and quickenings of unexpressed rivalries and doubts. And, most importantly, he can manage pauses without the audience losing its sense of continuing drama.

The pause marks silent interplay of conscious and unconscious motivation:

Bill. What time did you get in?
Harry. Four.
Bill. Good party?
Pause.
Harry. You didn't make any toast this morning.

Harry is "good" at parties; he answers the first question briefly because of his indulgence. Bill, whom he protects and to a certain extent supports, makes the reason for his own first question explicit in "Good party?" The pause then registers the hit. In the same moment, Harry feels guilty at his indulgence and so defends himself by attack. Probably none of these moves is calculated: but "something that escapes" these characters begins to "discover" the knowledge, feeling and reactions that lie beneath the trivial words. The pause enforces this discovery because it helps the audience to notice that Bill's second question remains unanswered. And the pause can be sustained without loss of audience interest because of the renewed energy and longer rhythm of Harry's return to dialogue.

The use of pauses is an important part of Hitchcock's technical vocabulary and perhaps Pinter learned something of its use there. (In *The Servant* and *Pumpkin Eater* he has written his first screenplays, while *The Caretaker* is now a film.) But the pause is also particularly useful in television, where the camera can hold attention in the enlarged intimacy of close-ups, and several of Pinter's plays started as television plays while others have been adapted for that medium with apparent ease. Thus his use of trivia accentuated by pauses is clearly linked with the major new art-forms of this century. By his musical and rhythmical control, he is able to dispense with the usual clarity and forward pressure of the narrative element of drama and so claim for the theatre some of the discoveries of films and television, and gain an enlargement of the little reactions that reveal man's unconscious life.

The trivial is especially revelatory when it is odd, when it seems like a funny mistake or even a conscious joke. (Freud discusses such revelations in *The Psychopathology of Everyday Life* [1901] and in *Jokes and their Relation to the Unconscious,* published four years later.) Here Pinter is a neo-realist, taking advantage of facts of human behaviour. He is fond of odd turns of conversation, odd habits of speech and odd mistakes. In *The Caretaker* Davies "forgets" that

Aston has given him money; he does not see that a gas stove is harmless when it is not connected; Aston fastens on the phrase "jig saw," rather than on "fret saw" or "hack saw." Unusual turns in the conversation sometimes lead to speeches of apparently disproportionate length: so Mick in *The Caretaker* recalls several people whom he knew, or says he knew, in other circumstances; or, in *The Collection,* James suddenly speaks of Hawkins, a "bloke" he "went to school with." Jokes are even more common. Pinter fastens on a pun or a trivial phrase with suggestive connotations, and then builds it into a joke. This is almost the manner of a music-hall song, like

> My daddy wouldn't buy me a bow-wow

or

> I always 'old with 'avin' it, if you fancy it,
> If you fancy it, that's understood.
> But if that's your bloomin' gime, I intend to do the sime
> 'Cause a little of what you fancy does yer good.

Marie Lloyd's song could be re-arranged as pinteresque dialogue and it is not surprising that in *The Dwarfs,* a radio play, Len asserts that Mark and Pete "are a music-hall act." In *The Birthday Party* McCann sings (*"in a full voice"*)

> Oh, the Garden of Eden has vanished, they say,
> But I know the lie of it still.

and this is immediately followed by a piece of dialogue with the repetition and developing innuendo of "I always 'old with 'avin' it":

> *Meg* (*rising*). I want to play a game!
> *Goldberg*. A game?
> *Lulu*. What game?
> *Meg*. Any game.
> *Lulu* (*jumping up*). Yes, let's play a game.
> *Goldberg*. What game?
> *McCann*. [*Who had sung of Eden.*] Hide and Seek.
> *Lulu*. Blind man's buff.
> *Meg*. Yes!
> *Goldberg*. You want to play blind man's buff?
> *Lulu and Meg*. Yes!

Goldberg acts here as a kind of stooge in the music-hall act, a feed: "What game? . . . You want to play blind man's buff?"; he gives the line so that others can bounce off it. (This effect is given an unusual interest in that Goldberg is also the most powerful, mysterious and [literally] large person on the stage; the leading music-hall performers may be the puppets of their "feed.")

Sometimes the humour of trivial conversation is less forcefully presented. In *The Lover* Richard speaks at first of the traffic he encounters on the way home with a hinted *double entendre* and only later makes this explicit. Almost any passage can seem to have a slight tilt towards physical and sexy suggestiveness or an exaggeration that only half-conceals mockery or fear. The milkman enters, in *The Lover,* to suggest Sarah's luxury in a repeated "Cream?", and an insistent "Don't you fancy any cream?" The talk of Mark's new suit in *The Dwarfs* has a run of words that tend to direct attention to Mark's body rather than its clothing: "zip at the hips . . . zip at the hips . . . buckle . . . turn-ups . . . turn-ups . . . turn-ups . . . double-breasted . . . double-breasted . . . double-breasted." In the breakfast-table duologue of *The Collection,* Harry has a pair of humorous exaggerations in "wonderful life" and "some maniac," that almost sharpens into a joke at his own or Bill's expense, and probably does so with the contrasted and unexpected 'He was shy.'

Occasionally Pinter uses a sharp verbal quibble, a jest that seems to express so much that it terminates a conversation; then he cuts, in a film-like way, to another scene. So in *The Collection* Bill has supposedly been telling James what truly happened between his (James's) wife and himself:

> *James.* Then I phoned.
> *Pause.*
> I spoke to her. Asked her how she was. She said she was all right. . . . She didn't have much to say. You were sitting on the bed next to her.
> *Silence.*
> *Bill.* Not sitting. Lying.
> *Blackout.*

Here Bill must enjoy the brevity of his "Lying" but then the scene at once shifts. Is he claiming a greater intimacy or is he confessing that he has told lies? The brief jest in a way not yet clear to the audience—it is not the end of the play—releases from Bill, perhaps unconsciously, his pleasure and momentary sense of being in command.

The way in which a single word may surprisingly yet humorously reveal hidden motives and recharge the dramatic situation can be illustrated from a reported speech in Freud's *The Psychopathology of Everyday Life,* where an old-fashioned stiffness of phrase sharpens attention on the device. Freud quotes a Dr. Dattner of Vienna:

> I was lunching in a restaurant with my colleague H., a doctor of philosophy. He spoke of the hardships of probationary students, and mentioned incidentally that before he had finished his studies he was given the post of secretary to the ambassador, or, more precisely, the minister plenipotentiary and extraordinary, of Chile. "But then [he said] the minister was transferred and I did not present myself to his successor". While he was uttering the last sentence he raised a piece of cake to his mouth, but let it drop from the knife in apparent clumsiness. I immediately grasped the hidden meaning of this symptomatic act, and, as it were casually, interjected to my colleague, who was unfamiliar with psycho-analysis: "You certainly allowed a tasty morsel to slip from you there". He . . . repeated my exact words with a peculiarly charming and surprising liveliness just as if my remark had taken the words out of his mouth: . . . and went on to unburden himself by means of a detailed description of the clumsiness which had lost him this well-paid position.

Here are Pinter's devices of repetition, suggestion, pun; so the trivial phrase reveals the Doctor of Philosophy's unspoken desire for fame and money. And so Meg, in *The Birthday Party,* asks if Stanley enjoyed the fried bread she has just given him and is really asking another question: "Was it nice?" "What?" "The fried bread." "Succulent." "You shouldn't say that word." "What word?" "That word you said." "What, succulent—?" "Don't say it!" "What's the matter with it?" "You shouldn't say that word to a married woman." The mistake of a word is the basic joke; and it is also an error that reveals.

Pinter is with Beckett in his use of jokes. In *Happy Days,* the emmet crawling on Winnie's mound is a diversion, a triviality with a joke about "formication"; and so it helps to reveal the shared qualities of Willie and Winnie. Or the trivial matter of Estragon's preference for carrots, over turnips and radishes, or for pink radishes over black ones, by repetition becomes funny and revealing: "this is becoming really insignificant" says Vladimir. But it is also a way of showing Estragon's self-centered and child-like concern for such physical matters and his rejoinder, "Not enough," emphasises this over against Vladimir's need to comprehend. By becoming laughably insignificant, the dialogue reveals significance.

Another characteristic that is basic to Pinter's dialogue has already been illustrated by the way: the exploitation of differences in the awareness of characters upon the stage. To Dr. Dattner his colleague was an interesting subject of investigation, while to the colleague Dr. Dattner was an amusing luncheon companion. Stanley was stating extravagantly that the fried bread was not very edible and to Meg he was almost making an improper suggestion. Life was getting tedious and undignified in Vladmir's consciousness, and it was lasting too long in Estragon's. Often the forward movement of Pinter's dialogue depends on the distance between the speakers' unexpressed awareness. So, when Harry says to Bill "You didn't make any toast this morning," he is unconsciously covering his own sense of guilt and Bill takes this as a challenge: "No. Do you want some?" At once this makes no real sense to Harry: he answers with apparent contradiction, "No. I don't." But Bill's mind continues with self-justification or an unconscious protest at his indebtedness to Harry: "I can if you like." But now Harry is no longer thinking about toast: "It's all right. Don't bother." Now he has forgotten entirely about the toast and also about challenging Bill; he half recognises the challenge in Bill's last speech and becomes lordly, perhaps covering-up with condescension. There is a pause and in it Harry's thought becomes more conscious so that he challenges Bill: "How are you spending your day today?".

Pinter not only writes dialogue that presents both conscious and unconscious thoughts behind the words but he is also adept at keeping several flows of consciousness alive in a single conversation and making them apparent to the audience. Again he is in company with other writers; notably with Chekhov. He is also asking actors to sustain a kind of illusion that has been considered radically by Stanislavski. (The help it gives in identifying "subtext" beneath the words of a play is one of the reasons why "The Method" has become so ubiquitous in twentieth-century theatres.) Subtext in Stanislavski's own definition implies the consciousness

> beneath the words of the text, giving them life and a basis for existing . . . a web of innumerable, varied inner patterns . . . all sorts of figments of the imagination, inner movements, objects of attention, smaller and greater truths and a belief in them, adaptations, adjustments and other similar elements. It is the subtext that makes us say the words we do in a play.

Such a concept will help an actor to recognise the importance of presenting the apparent trivialities of Pinter's dialogue with an inward, or subconscious, accuracy.

Many exercises used for training in The Method aim at developing divergent awarenesses within a duologue. Here is part of a very elementary acting-class described by Stanislavski: "Now make this test. What response do you give to the words in your ears, 'Let's go to the station!'?" The instructor is speaking, and then Stanislavski describes the reactions of the pupils, including himself:

> I saw myself leaving the house, taking a cab, driving through certain streets, crossing avenues and soon found myself inside the railway station. Leo thought of himself as pacing up and down a platform, whereas Sonya's thoughts had already allowed her to flit off to southern climes and visit several resorts.
>
> (*Building a Character* [ed. 1950], p. 116.)

Words can send different minds to different destinations in place and, very important, in time. Pinter is continually concerned with this, and much of the life of his dialogue derives from the subtle indications—through trivial matters often—of such divergencies.

Pinter's reliance on multiple and conflicting subtexts poses the main problem for understanding his dialogue, especially in reading the mere words of the printed text. He has said that:

> The speech we hear is an indication of that we don't hear. It is a necessary avoidance, a violent, sly, anguished or mocking smoke-screen which keeps the other in its place.
>
> ('Between the Lines', *The Sunday Times* [4 March, 1962], p. 25.)

On the printed page we read the smoke-screen; we can analyse the diversionary tactics of two commanders who are sometimes unaware of the combat that is taking place. Even actors find the dialogue difficult—even Pinter himself. In a report of rehearsals for *The Collection* something can be learnt of appropriate ways for understanding the demands of the words upon the actors. Pinter was directing for Peter Hall at the Aldwych:

> "I'm probably complicating things," he said to John Ronane, a young actor, "but it's worth complicating. We haven't really ever quite examined this speech, have we? Until we find out what it means to you, there can't be any real . . . You know?" Pinter coughed and took off his glasses. "We have to find . . . Don't be worried."
>
> "I'm not worried", said Ronane. "I'm just completely—lost."

The report continues:

> "Pinter sat down and took pains to discuss exactly what he wanted from an actor."

"The thing is, Harold's plays take such bloody concentration," Kenneth Haigh is reported to have said to Barbara Murray—that is, the James to the Stella. A piece of duologue in the text runs:

> —Tall, was he?
> —That's . . . what he was.

and at this point Pinter stopped the rehearsal: "I find this a little too. . . ." "Open?" "Yes, yes, yes. It could be a very nasty . . . . Well, yes, I think it needs a split second. . . . I think it can take that." He explained, too, that when Harry says to Stella "Oh, what a beautiful lamp!" he is avoiding saying what he is thinking. In literal terms it is a lie; he doesn't like the lamp: "Michael, you see," said Pinter to Michael Hordern, "it's not your taste at all. The whole thing's horrid." Harry in the play is not talking about the lamp, in fact; he is responding to Stella. ('Taking Pains with Pinter,' *The Observer* [10 June, 1962], p. 19.)

Reading Pinter's dialogue needs, in the first instance, concentration. Every detail, and especially the odd, funny, suggestive, repeated, the "really insignificant," has to be scrutinized to see what it "means," subtextually; our appreciation is "worth complicating."

In all this, care must be given to consistency; earlier in *The Collection* it has been made obvious that Harry has an immaculate and severe taste for period furnishing and collects Chinese porcelain; and that Stella's flat is in what is called "tasteful contemporary furnishing." Most importantly the plays must be read backwards if their words are to be understood fully. At the end of *The Caretaker* Pinter required that one of the two people in the room "must go in such a way as to produce a sense of complete separation and finality": the smoke-screens have cleared away and everything in some way, perhaps only through apparently trivial matters, has been said between them. It was this statement of character towards which Aston and Davies had been, with every show of clumsiness, moving relentlessly. To understand the earlier dialogue with all its subtextual complexities it is necessary to recognise that Davies is dependent and Aston aspirant:

> If you want me to go . . . I'll go. You just say the word.
>
> *Pause.*
>
> I'll tell you what though . . . them shoes . . . them shoes you give me . . . they're working out all right . . . they're all right. Maybe I could . . . get down . . . .
>
> *Ashton remains still, his back to him, at the window.*
>
> Listen . . . If I . . . got down . . . if I was to . . . get my papers . . . would you . . . would you let . . . would you . . . if I got down . . . and got my . . . .
>
> *Long silence.*
>
> *Curtain.*

In the light of this moment, we can learn the subtextual importance of all the earlier and—then—baffling talk of coming and going, of shoes, work, giving, buying, fighting, bric-a-brac, Sidcup, the weather, and of the site for a hut in the overgrown garden visible from the single window.

At the end of *The Collection* before the characters reassume the positions they occupied at the beginning of the play, James has been with Bill and Harry with Stella, a re-arrangement that had come about instinctively, or subtextually; if this movement is to have credibility, the energies that caused it must have been suggested, however lightly, under the earlier words and actions.

Again a further characteristic of Pinter's dialogue has already been illustrated. At the end of *The Caretaker* Aston's response to the stream of words from Davies does not include any words at all. He looks out of the window and the audience knows that this is towards the garden where he wishes to build with his own hands a wooden hut. Then the final confrontation of the two characters is silence from both of them, and stillness. This is typical: Pinter's dialogue intimately relates words and gestures and often progresses from words to gestures.

Stanley in *The Birthday Party* is, like Davies, a man of many words. He can readily describe his day-dreams of a reception with champagne or of a youth spent in a "quiet, thriving community," and he can insult his landlady accurately. But when Pinter wishes to show Stanley's deeper, inarticulate feelings at the end of Act I, he gives him action rather than speech:

> *He hangs the drum around his neck, taps it gently with the sticks, then marches round the table, beating it regularly.* MEG, *pleased, watches him. Still beating it regularly, he begins to go round the table a second time. Halfway round the beat becomes erratic, uncontrolled.* MEG *expresses dismay. He arrives at her chair, banging the drum, his face and the drumbeat now savage and possessed.*

This is very much a contemporary dramatic device. In a more conventional play, the dramatist often seems to abdicate to his actors for the climax of a scene, as in the stage-direction at the end of the second Act of John Osborne's *Look Back in Anger:*

> *She slaps his face savagely. An expression of horror and disbelief floods his face. But it drains away, and all that is left is pain. His hand goes up to his head, and a muffled cry of despair escapes him. Helena tears his hand away, and kisses him passionately, drawing him down beside her.*

Here there is no drum to give size to the incident or extend the time of its duration. The actor must try to catch the proper expression of "horror and disbelief" and then let it "drain away" to leave only "pain"; and he must catch the attention of the audience with this merely facial play. A less adventurous or more practised dramatist will at least devise some large movements to help the performer, as at the end of Scene ii in *Table by the Window* in Rattigan's *Separate Tables*:

> JOHN *stands looking down at her for a moment, then suddenly throws her to the floor in front of the fireplace. The coffee table is overturned.* JOHN *goes to the french windows, pulls them open and runs out. The wind blows the curtains into the room.* ANNE *lies quite still for a few moments, her face expressionless, then she gets up, sobbing, turns to the fireplace and stares at herself for a long time in the mirror over the mantelpiece. She turns quickly away, sobs quietly at first, and then more violently, until, as she makes her way blindly to the arch up R, it is uncontrollable.* MISS COOPER *enters up R, . . .*

Here the dramatist conducts his actress, moment by moment, through a sustained climax of movement and gesture. But Pinter tries to make action still more eloquent. He does not introduce stage business because he has a situation he cannot handle precisely, but because it has developed beyond words: it needs concentration, surprise, strong rhythm, noise, instinctiveness, physical relief and activity, metaphorical reverberations. For Pinter gesture is a precise and powerful expression, not a way of passing the whole play over to the actor; it is a language which he tries to make precise.

This obvious experimentation can be parallelled in the works of other writers. In *The Three Sisters* Soliony is always perfuming and cleansing his hands or, nearer Pinter's own day, Ann Jellicoe's *Sport of My Mad Mother* has a scene where Caldaro is knocked out and wrapped up in newspaper by a gang of Teds. The author herself has commented in an interview in *The New Theatre Magazine*, (1960):

> in this action there are hardly any words that make sense—there's nothing which your intellect can take in. If you sit watching and say "What does this *mean*? What does this *mean*?" you're not going to get anywhere; but if you allow yourself to be excited by the visual action and the gradual crescendo of noise underlining this, you may begin to appreciate what it's *about*.

By such devices Miss Jellicoe has centred her drama on group sensations, showing the pathos and potential power of a band of illiterates. In contrast Ionesco uses stage business to give visual form to the fantasies of individual characters. His actions are often strange and exaggerated: a corpse grows longer and longer in *Amédée,* as the hero's sense of guilt increases, and the wife in *Victims of Duty* expresses her apprehension and feelings of inadequacy by silently bringing countless cups of coffee to placate the Detective or the other characters who seem to threaten her home. In *The New Tenant* gesture stops the play by literally filling the whole stage: its titular hero wants to feel "really at home" and so orders himself to be surrounded by his furniture; this is enacted, more and more properties being placed around him, until he is firmly imprisoned and only the light has to be put out to complete the play's action. For Ionesco, as for Pinter, stage properties extend the silent language of gesture and present the fearful and ludicrous reality of dreams and subconscious conflicts.

Such gestures are sensational and of forceful impact, but Pinter, and with him Beckett, have also discovered how to link gestures with dialogue so that they make a more subtle impression. The point can be so fine that a gesture has to be repeated frequently or sustained for a long time. McCann in *The Birthday Party* twice sits down to tear sheets of newspaper into equal strips. The first time he does so the audience may see only an intriguing piece of business but McCann subsequently rebukes Stanley for touching the strips and in the third Act his fearful concentration in tearing more newspaper communicates itself to Goldberg and its effect is to bring upon McCann a revealingly angry rebuke. McCann has been concentrating his attention; this expresses a need to escape from consciousness of fears. In Beckett's *Waiting for Godot,* Vladimir fiddles with his hat, at first inexplicably; but with repetition this becomes an expression of the uncertainty of his attempt to live by conscious effort. Estragon's repeated struggles with his boots show, by the end of the play, how he becomes individually responsible through pain. These gestures are no larger than ordinary behaviour but are slightly odd; they need explanation, and the audience is encouraged to consider them like puzzles until the slow exposition of the play reveals the inner need that actuates, explains and gives power to them.

A mere presence on stage without words has become a favourite 'gesture' of dramatists. During the opening duologue of *The Collec-*

tion Bill *"looks at"* Harry in silence. This action is an inextricable part of the confrontation: the fact that Bill does not answer the violent word "maniac" with any word at all expresses his consciousness. During the *"look,"* in association with words and their accentuation of the pause, Pinter has expressed a shade of response that could not be communicated by words.

In the nineteen-twenties Jean-Jacques Bernard developed a "theatre of silence" to display inarticulate sentiments, and Chekhov in *The Seagull* of 1896 had ended his play with long pauses as Constantin tears manuscripts and the family silently play at the card table. These were monumental silences, given unambiguous meaning by the narrative. In Bernard's *Martine,* for example, the audience reaches the moment of silence, when Martine confronts Julien for the last time, fully and directly informed of its meaning:

> Don't tremble, Martine! . . . There's nothing wrong in what I'm saying to you . . . It's not a sin to think tenderly of the past . . . for a moment . . . (*His voice softens*) For a moment . . .
> (*Impulsively, his eyes pleading, he holds out his arms.* MARTINE *is trembling, scared, her eyes wild*)
> No, no, don't tremble . . . .
> (*He moves towards her.* MARTINE *sways slightly to him, ashamed, yet already giving herself to the moment*)
> Martine . . . Martine . . . (*And suddenly he seems to pause. His eyes are uneasy, compunctious. Slowly he drops his arms . . . Confused, and awkward, he merely takes her hand*) Before I go . . . I . . . I hope you'll be happy, Martine . . . (*He walks away abruptly*)
> (MARTINE *is left standing by the table, her breast heaving as she fights back her sobs)*
> (*Between his teeth*) What came over me? . . . What have I been saying? . . .
> (*So they remain for a moment, without speaking.* JULIEN *is biting his knuckles . . .* JEANNE *comes in from the street. She is in deep mourning.*)
> *Jeanne.* We're all ready, Julien.

This climax in the presentation of Martine is clarified by all the preceding narrative and by Julien's stumbling verbal comments which punctuate the silent gestures. In *The Seagull* Dorn directly announces that Constantin has shot himself. At the end of *Uncle*

Vania there is a silence for which the audience may be unprepared, but then both Vania and Sonia make the inarticulate explicit:

> *Marina.* He's gone.
> (*A pause.*)
> *Sonia.* (*Comes back and puts the candle on the table.*) He's gone.
> *Vania.* (*Counts on the abacus and writes down.*) Total . . . fifteen . . . twenty-five . . .
> *Marina.* (*Yawns.*) Lord forgive us our sins . . .
> (*Telyeghin enters on tiptoe, sits down by the door and quietly tunes his guitar.*)

This is a silent tableau and then:

> *Vania.* (*To Sonia, passing his hand over her hair.*) My child, there's such a weight on my heart! Oh, if only you knew how much my heart aches!
> *Sonia.* Well, what can we do? We must go on living!
> (*A pause.*)
> We shall go on living, Uncle Vania. We shall live through a long, long succession of days and tedious evenings. We shall patiently suffer the trials which Fate imposes on us; . . .

And so on: the play soon ends with Sonia's assertion that they will be peaceful after death. Here, at last, everything has been stated in words, whereas in *Godot* or *The Caretaker* the "brief tableau" of silence and stillness is the concluding impression.

The originality of Pinter and other dramatists writing today lies in their belief that gesture can be as eloquent as words. In this some have been encouraged by the prophecies of Antonin Artaud. In *The Theatre and its Double* he has written about a drama very different from all except his own productions and Genet's texts, but some of his theories sound generally applicable:

> I make it my principle that words do not mean everything and that by their nature and defining character, fixed once and for all, they arrest and paralyse thought instead of permitting it and fostering its development.

He has asked for a "concrete language" that is independent of speech, claiming that

> there is a poetry of the senses as there is a poetry of language, and that this concrete physical language to which I refer is truly theatrical

only to the degree that the thoughts it expresses are beyond the reach of the spoken language.

Such a physical language seems a necessity today. We understand that no man can be judged solely by the thoughts and feelings he can speak about and recognize: he is what he is by virtue of his unknown desires and needs as well. Recognising this more clearly than earlier generations, dramatists look for a mirror to hold up to human nature that can reflect the unspoken and the unspeakable with more clarity of form and continuance of pressure than dialogue of statement or the indirect dialogue of apparent insignificance. Pinter's "dialogue" contains gestures as well as words, must be seen as well as heard.

In his use of the physical language of stage-business Pinter is in a wide stream of dramatic experiment. Almost every dramatist writing today is concerned to some extent with the same problem. In *Look Back in Anger* (1956) John Osborne directed Alison to stand mutely ironing while Jim shows off his aggressive nature. In *Chin-Chin* (1960) Billetdoux made the mutual gesture of two people drinking together an image of their personal relationship explored by the whole play; it is accompanied by only a tired repeated phrase. Arnold Wesker reveals the strength of Peter's resentment at his way of life in *The Kitchen* (performed 1959) by making him seize a chopper to break open a gas pipe. Tennessee Williams in *Rose Tattoo* (1950) had Serafina run into the garden holding a pink silk shirt *"above her head defiantly"*; she drops it with only *"a soft cry"* and then it is snatched away by other women so that it is *"like a streak of flame shooting up a dry hill."* In *Flowering Cherry* (1957), Robert Bolt's hero bends an iron poker on several occasions because the gesture represents his dream of a better life than his own. In each of these plays gesture is subservient to the text, but the need to devise a new kind of eloquence is clearly recognized. Williams tried to underline the effect of his action by an accompaniment of music beginning *"with a crash of percussion,"* Bolt by directing

The music of the "Flowering Cherry" theme is heard. The lights fade except for a spot on Cherry [*the hero*] *and the vision lighting* [*of a Somerset orchard in full blossom*] *comes slowly up.*

Pinter's individual achievement in this respect is the complex interplay of his words and actions. The crude device of the drum in *The Birthday Party* is exceptional. His later characters still play with drums as in *The Lover,* or with knives or a white kitten as in *The Collection,* but Pinter no longer tries to overwhelm with a single gesture. The presentation of characters in their various modes of conscious and unconscious existence is achieved by many touches, each deft and precise. Now the final gesture can be a slight confrontation:

> *Long silence.*
> JAMES *leaves the house.*
> HARRY *sits.* BILL *remains sitting sucking his hand.*
> *Silence.*
> *Fade house to half light.*
> *Fade up full on flat.*
> STELLA *is lying with the kitten.*
> *The flat door closes.* JAMES *comes in. He stands looking at her.*

Then after a few more words:

> STELLA *looks at him, neither confirming nor denying. Her face is friendly, sympathetic.*
> *Fade flat to half light.*
> *The four figures are still, in the half light.*
> *Fade to blackout.*
>
> *Curtain.*

At the end of *The Lover* there is a drum, but it has been seen before and now the tangled fingers express the physical proximity of Richard and Sarah.

Pinter's originality is to be found in his style, and the aim of his style is to reveal the varying consciousness of his characters; to understand all he writes and assess his achievement it is necessary to look through the web of conversation and gesture to notice the other slowly-moving patterns underneath.

Even the interest of a play's action is here dependent on the half-hidden nature of the characters' moment-by-moment involvement. It was once said that *The Birthday Party* is a play with an exciting situation that is never developed. This is true in conventional terms, for despite its brief story the main effect is to give a developing knowledge of the characters. In all the plays, any slight change of situation serves to effect a change in the audience's awareness, to make half-perceived revelations click into place. Pinter's dialogue is contrived, so that, when a radically new situation is at last presented, the audience has already sensed the subtle and slow-developing movements which make it inevitable. (This is why actors have to take pains to be consistent, to study their whole parts in order to discover how to play any one moment.) If the final tableau seems right and necessary to the audience, Pinter's whole design has worked: the action and dialogue have the same inner compulsion.

This fatefulness expressed in a play's action is not considered directly in words, but its effectiveness is inescapable if the actors have achieved any degree of success. And, to help them, Pinter has persistently maintained an intimation of the un-named forces behind the fashionable, accurate, amusing, everyday, trivial talk. The whole design is inextricably concerned with psychological issues, but that is not all. Each concluding change of situation comes with an added awareness in the characters of some previously hidden bias (as in *A Slight Ache* or *The Lover*), or with the elimination of other responses (as with Aston in *The Caretaker*), or with violence (as in *The Dumb-Waiter* when Gus enters beaten-up or in *The Room* when Rose is blinded). In creating his complex dialogue and shapely plays, Pinter has found a means of showing a world of apparent triviality and helplessness that must find a closer and stronger truth in human relationships, or else must submit to violence and challenge; only in these ways can his plays end.

Pinter's drama has something of the rigorous dissection of Strindberg. It has more of that enlargement of the usual to gain both revelation and entertainment which is found, variously, in Freud, Beckett and Music-Hall performances. But this dramatist is no showman or lecturer; he does not comment, or sum up, or stop for applause. He relies above all on the deeply considered expressiveness of actors who are used to the scrutiny of film or television cameras and also willing to 'complicate' their performances. Stanislavski's training techniques would be wholly applicable for actors in Pinter's plays as in Chekhov's, but more depends on them; no other dramatist of subtle character portrayal, including Ibsen and Shakespeare, has made psychological expressiveness so entirely the central fact and actuating principle of his drama.

The gains are paradoxical. The *dramatis personae* have become more normal, inhabiting the author's and actor's own mental and emotional world, so that any strangeness in the action seems like a representation of familiar fantasy and any violence a realisation of an unconsidered fear of violation. And at the same time the characters seem more imprisoned in conditions established before the play began and in the lack of any intellectually conceived means of escape; even the brief and fated development of their situations is inextricably predicated in all the petty decisions they make towards speech or action. On first hearing, or on impatient acquaintance, Pinter's plays, like his dialogue, can seem banal; their size, colour, delicacy and weight depend on the actors' ability to transmit under the text the deep and necessarily consistent truth of behaviour that they discovered in long rehearsal. If this is achieved in performance the author's world can become that of his audience, and his search for power and stability (or "truth") can enlighten its imagination.[1]

[1] Translations used in this article are: Antonin Artaud, *The Theater and Its Double,* trans. Mary C. Richards (1958); Jean-Jacques Bernard, *The Sulky Fire; Five Plays,* trans. J. L. Frith (1939); Anton Chekhov, *Plays,* trans. Elizaveta Fen (1959); Sigmund Freud, *The Complete Psychological Works,* Vol. vi, trans. J. Strachey (1960); Constantin Stanislavski, *Building a Character,* trans. Elizabeth R. Hapgood (1950).

The Homecoming: Kith and Kin

by Hugh Nelson

Without exception, Harold Pinter's plays have titles which seem neither enigmatic nor evocative. Casually scanned, they seem not to merit a second look, since they simply abstract a central object, person, or event from the context of the play. This is again true of his most recent play, *The Homecoming*. The title would seem at first glance to indicate nothing but the central event around which the action pivots, or, to put it in the terminology of the well-made play, its inciting incident.

In the first act, the stage is set for the bizarre but logical consequences of the second act. We see a family, two pairs of brothers a generation apart, a family which has a certain routine of daily living. Within this routine, signs of strain and stress are writ large. Max and his son Lenny are involved in a predatory struggle for dominance. Unable to conquer Lenny, Max turns on his own brother, Sam, a fellow creature less capable of offering direct resistance, and impugns his masculinity on the one hand while accusing him of being a secret lecher on the other. Joey, Lenny's brother, is treated with a mixture of condescension and coddling. A boxer and a demolition worker, he appears to have the physical means at hand to dominate all of them, but a certain slow-wittedness prevents his taking the opportunities available to him.

In earlier Pinter plays, we have become accustomed to seeing family situations in which such stresses were apparent. We have also become accustomed to seeing these stresses revealed through the small rituals of family living: breakfasts, tea, dusting, opening and closing windows, repairing broken stair rods and leaks in the ceiling. Pinter is interested in these trivia not for their own sake but for the opportunities they afford him to expose much deeper states of unrest, boredom, and resentment. In *The Homecoming,* the same technique is used. Max is furious because he has to fix dinner for his family: "Honest. They walk in here every time of the day and night like bloody animals. Go and find yourself a mother." [1] Lenny criticizes his cooking: "You're a dog cook. Honest. You think you're cooking for a lot of dogs." Apparent inconsequence always comes home to roost in Pinter. After the homecomers have come home, Max makes several crucial inquiries of his oldest son's wife:

Max. You a mother?
Ruth. Yes.
Max. How many you got?
Ruth. Three.

* * *

Max. I've got the feeling you're a first rate cook.
Ruth. I'm not bad.
Max. No, I've got the feeling you're a number one cook. Am I right, Teddy?
Teddy. Yes, she's a very good cook.

The real problem then is that the family we see at the beginning of the play is womanless, hence unbalanced, out of phase. There is no cook, no mother, no sexual partner, or, rather, inadequate substitutes for all of these necessities. Max is the cook at night and Sam the cook in the morning; neither is happy with his role; both the feeders and the fed use this issue to "get at" each other. In place of the woman they need, they have a memory, Max's late wife, Jessie. From the various descriptions we get of her, she seems to have been all things to all men. Sam speaks of her with reverence but reveals at a climactic moment that he had acted as her procuror. Max speaks of her as an ideal wife and mother at one moment; and the next, she becomes a "slutbitch." Eventually, Ruth, the intruder, will also find

[1] All quotes from *The Homecoming* were originally drawn from an unpublished manuscript which I wish to thank Mr. Harold Pinter for the privilege of reading and the permission to quote from. The last speech quoted, from "Well, if that's the kind of thing . . ." to "Is that what you've given us?", occurs in a different version in the published text; all other quotations conform in essentials to the printed version.

herself compelled to take on such apparently opposed tasks and roles, but not until she has fathomed the family and its needs and, in turn, been fathomed by them.

The homecoming initiates the forward movement. Teddy and Ruth arrive late at night. There are clear indications of stress and imbalance in their relationship as well. Ruth wants to go out for a walk; Teddy demurs, then goes out for a walk himself. Lenny appears, draws his own conclusions, and operates on them. His acceptance of Ruth as Teddy's wife is perfunctory at best. Clearly, he sees something more in her. She sees that he sees and brings the issue to him. (As Edward says of the Matchseller in *A Slight Ache*: "The man's an impostor and he knows I know it. . . . And I know he knows I know it. . . . And he knows I know.") Again, the means is trivial, a glass of water. But the subtext is loaded:

> *Ruth.* Have a sip. Go on. Have a sip from my glass. Sit on my lap. Take a long cool sip. Put your head back and open your mouth.
> *Lenny.* Take that glass away from me.
> *Ruth.* Lie on the floor. Go on. I'll pour it down your throat.
> *Lenny.* What are you doing, making me some kind of proposal?

The following morning, Ruth and Teddy, two ethereal apparitions in dressing gowns, come downstairs with the family morning in full career. Max decides that Ruth is a whore. After taking out his violence on Sam and Joey, he greets the returning prodigal and his new daughter-in-law in a curtain scene dripping with sarcasm. Like Lenny, he is not so easily dislodged from his first conclusions.

The second act is a shocker, but those critics, like Walter Kerr, who have implied that it could or should stand by itself as a one-act play are misled. None of the events in this act would be supportable without the first act foundation. It is also important to see that the central movement of this act and of the play is Ruth's process of self-discovery. Teddy's victimization and his presumably lonely return to America and to the fall semester are only of peripheral interest. In addition, the play does not seem to be about the victimization of Ruth. At its conclusion, she is the queen bee, as Flora is at the end of *A Slight Ache,* as Meg is at the end of *The Birthday Party,* as Stella is at the conclusion of *The Collection.* It is a much stronger play when viewed as a process of self-discovery in which

Ruth remembers things about herself, discovers things she had not known, weighs the needs of Teddy against those of the group, and makes an amoral but none the less logical choice. Max, Lenny, and Joey may have a certain hypnotic effect upon her, but it is a hypnosis which she chooses to undergo. (Stanley's "victimization" in *The Birthday Party* should be viewed in the same way as pointed up by Petey's poignant warning: "Stan, don't let them tell you what to do.")

But we, the audience, need more time to evaluate the strength of needs than Ruth, the character, does. Thus, the first act is crucial in allowing us to see the motherless, wifeless, sexless family in operation and in allowing us to see the essential sterility of Ruth's relationship to Teddy (three children notwithstanding). Her description of America is telling: "It's all rock. And sand. It stretches . . . so far . . . everywhere you look. And there's lots of insects there. (*Pause.*) And there's lots of insects there." The only vision that Teddy can muster with which to hold her is one of swimming pools and lecture halls. This is not enough. Teddy's "intellectual equilibrium" upon which he prides himself finally excludes Ruth as well as his "blood" family: "You're just objects. You just . . . move about. I can observe it. I can see what you do. It's the same as I do. But you're lost in it. You won't get me being . . . I won't be lost in it." Ruth chooses to lose herself and, like the Biblical prodigal, is found. Or, rather, she finds herself—as mother, whore, manageress, cook, housekeeper, and brood mare. Very early in the play, Max had mentioned his way with horses, particularly the fillies:

> But I was always able to tell a good filly by one particular trick. I'd look her in the eye. You see? I'd stand in front of her and look her straight in the eye, it was a kind of hypnotism, and by the look deep down in her eye I could tell whether she was a stayer or not. It was a gift. I had a gift.

In the play's final moments, Max tries to fathom the Ruth they have helped to bring to life and finds that his "gift" has deserted him.

Thus, the title of the play, seemingly obvious, must be re-examined. Again, this is true of all of Pinter's plays. "The birthday party" is a central event in the play which bears its name, but it is much more than a birthday party; it is also an initiation and a rebirth.

"The dumb waiter" is a physical object and a state of being. "The caretaker" is a specific function offered to Davies and also a deep pun on man's responsibility for his fellow man. "The homecoming" like "the birthday party" is an event that occurs in the play: Teddy comes home. But the truer of the "homecomings" is Ruth's. She comes home to herself, to all of her possibilities as a woman. What she comes home to may not be very pleasant and the experience of watching the return may be lacerating, but in Pinter's world, as in that of Sophoclean tragedy or in the equally fatal universe of Ibsen, the human truth will always out. In fact, it is interesting that Pinter's titles are similar to those of the early Ibsen. As titles, *A Doll's House, Ghosts, Pillars of Society,* and *The Master Builder* have a double-edged ironic thrust to which Pinter's titles simply add an ingrained affinity for the play on words.

II

Pinter has frequently referred to himself as an extremely traditional playwright. This warning has generally been ignored. In the fashionable rush to see him as a playwright of the "absurd" (whatever that may mean) or as Chekhov's heir in the contemporary theatre, it is seldom realized that his form may be closer to the well-made play in its Ibsenite incarnation than to any other structural source. In a recent interview, he was quoted as saying:

> I *am* a very traditional playwright—for instance I insist on having a curtain in all of my plays. I write curtain lines for that reason. . . . For me everything has to do with shape, structure, and over-all unity.[2]

The Homecoming an Ibsenite play? Only if we see that exposition, development, and resolution have been driven underground through a healthy distrust of language. The surface of any one of Pinter's plays may seem chaotic, arbitrary, and illogical. Short passages of stichomythia about apparently irrelevant subjects may be succeeded by massive speeches recounting personal experience, plans, dreams, bus routes which seem not to fit into the context in which they appear. This pattern is even truer of *The Homecoming* in which

[2] Interview with Lawrence Bensky abstracted from the forthcoming issue of *The Paris Review*. Quoted from *The New York Times* (January 1, 1967).

Pinter's increased daring in the manipulation of dramatic dialogue is readily apparent. But to react to this dialogue as arbitrary absurdity is to miss the true excitement of a Pinter play. For in Pinter, far more than in many playwrights credited with tightness of construction and dramatic economy, every word is chosen so that in the final analysis, nothing in the design shall seem arbitrary. Apparently trivial differences of opinion over cheese rolls, cigars, glasses of water, routes to the airport, are, in fact, Pinter's somewhat unique means of exposition and development. What we lack in precise information about the characters' backgrounds and motives is made up for by a very complex knowledge (if we are alert to it) of the nature of their shifting emotions in regard to each other. What they do *not* say becomes as important here as what they do say. Thus, the pause, the silence, can take on an expository and developmental function. In addition, there are physical indicators. Pinter has stated that he begins his plays with a vision of certain physical relationships between people in a room: sitting, standing, lying, kneeling. A careful look at his final curtains will reveal a significantly altered physical relationship which makes a statement beyond the power of words. Other individual moments allow us to chart stages in the development again by purely physical means.

The Homecoming with its sinister family history (*à la Rosmersholm*), its clear division between exposition and development incited by the homecoming (*à la Ghosts*), its withheld facts from the past suddenly revealed in a climactic scene (*à la* almost any Ibsen play), and its emphatic resolution, is structurally a very traditional piece of playwrighting. What Pinter mainly adds is a distrust of language, a belief that language is more often used as evasion than as revelation. Only if we are committed to charting structural unity in a play through what is said, only if we are unwilling to try to see through layers of subterfuge to the emotional truth of individual moments, shall we be induced to believe that the structure of the play is arbitrary or that deliberate obfuscation is a motivating force.

In Pinter, development is internalized. In his earliest play, *The Room,* we are only mystified by the events that occur if we fail to realize that what we see on the stage is the gradual revelation of one character's inner life, her inner geography, first through monologue, later through the dramatic action itself. We are first given hints about her fears, her conflicting desires for security and for knowledge, which the action, culminating in the appearance of a mysterious blind visitor, forces into the open where she must make a decision. As Pinter's technique has developed, he has eschewed approaching his material through the inner life of a single character and has worked towards a balance in which various individual needs and fears may all be answered, if not satisfied, by a single resolution. The major turning point came in Act Three of *The Birthday Party*, where Pinter, having disposed of his ostensible hero, moved on to examine the conflicting needs of the group which had disposed of the victim. But the concept of inner geography remains valid in the subsequent plays. Exposition, development, and resolution can not be open in Pinter because he refuses to compel any character to say more than he wants to say or can say at a given moment. But what the characters do say is always to the point in that it exposes more and more what the characters fear, anticipate, and cherish. In this respect, it often does not matter whether what they say is, in fact, true. An invented past can be as telling as a true one. Thus, it makes little difference whether Ruth was or wasn't a photographic model for the body, or whether she was or wasn't a whore when Teddy married her. It makes little difference whether Jessie did or didn't sleep with MacGregor, whether Lenny's stories of his violence towards women are highly exaggerated or complete fabrications, or whether Teddy and Ruth have three children or not. The play does not operate at a level of facts. As Pinter has said: "The desire for verification is understandable but cannot always be satisfied." [3] All we are to expect from the play is a gradually expanding knowledge of the inner lives of the characters. This knowledge almost always reveals an imbalance which we can count on the resolution to bring to a new equilibrium. Pinter's vision of human relationships is basically dialectical. Contradictions lead to new syntheses which in turn may break apart. While the family is discussing Ruth's new position and making plans for an advertising campaign to put the product across, Teddy interjects a telling reservation:

[3] Program note for performances of *The Room* and *The Dumb Waiter*, Royal Court Theatre, London, March, 1960.

Teddy. She'd get old very quickly.

Max. No . . . not in this day and age! With the health service? Old! How could she get old?

The resolution of *The Homecoming* is not to be taken as final, but it has resolved one set of contradictions.

The play is full of extraordinary moments. One of the most striking is Sam's last-minute revelation which seems for a moment to have provoked his decease:

Sam. (*in one breath*) MacGregor had Jessie in the back of my cab as I drove them along. (*He croaks and collapses. . . .*)

Max. What's he done? Dropped dead?

Lenny. Yes.

Max. A corpse? A corpse on my floor? Get him out of here! Clear him out of here!

Joey. He's not dead.

Lenny. He probably was dead, for about thirty seconds.

Max. He's not even dead!

This scene interrupts the forward momentum of the dramatic action, the snowballing plans for setting Ruth up in business and for "finalizing" the deal. A moment later, the participants return to the business at hand leaving Sam to remain stretched on the carpet (dead or alive) until the final curtain. What is this but proof reasonably positive of some of the points made above? It is the old Scribean *scene à faire* wedged into a situation where death becomes a farce. Poor Sam's carefully concealed fact, his delayed exposition, his last-minute message, is of no importance and never was of any importance. The characters have made their decisions on the basis of what each wishes to remember of the past, what each wants to see in the present, what each needs, desires, and fears. That decision is inevitable, irrevocable. For his trouble, Sam gets an abbreviated eulogy:

Max. You know what that man had?

Lenny. Has.

Max. Has! A diseased imagination.

III

> And Ruth said, intreat me not to leave thee, or to return from following after thee: for whither you

goest, I will go; and where thou lodgest, I will lodge: thy people shall be my people, and thy God my God.

The Book of Ruth, I.16

And he arose and came to his father. But when he was yet a great way off, his father saw him, and had compassion, and ran, and fell on his neck and kissed him. And the son said unto him, Father, I have sinned against heaven, and in thy sight, and am no more worthy to be called thy son. But the father said to his servants, Bring forth the best robe, and put it on him; and put a ring on his hand, and shoes on his feet: And bring hither the fatted calf, and kill it; and let us eat and be merry: For this my son was dead, and is alive again; he was lost, and is found. And they began to be merry.

St. Luke, XV. 20-24

Bi-fold authority! Where reason can revolt
Without perdition, and loss assumes all reason
Without revolt: This is and is not Cressid!
Within my soul there doth conduce a fight
Of this strange nature, that a thing inseparate
Divides more wider than the sky and earth;
And yet the spacious breadth of this division
Admits no orifex for a point as subtle
As Ariachna's broken woof to enter.

Troilus and Cressida, v.ii.141-49

There are two frames of reference in Pinter's plays which have not been sufficiently explored, the Biblical (or Judaic) and the Shakespearean. The influence of the strictly modern, particularly of Beckett and Ionesco and their literary forbears, Kafka, Proust, and Joyce, carries us a certain distance into the early plays, although from the very beginning Pinter is doing absolutely unique and personal things and, in many ways, is in complete contrast to Ionesco's techniques and aims.

Pinter's statements about his methods seem to indicate a controlled but essentially intuitive approach:

I merely write and characters create themselves. I don't arbitrarily impose a characterisation upon someone, and say you're going to be

> like this to prove a point that I'm going to make. The stage opens, the curtain goes up and characters move along with it.[4]

Such an approach is even more open than normally to a certain degree of unconscious influence based on deeper layers of background and experience. Two vital facts in Pinter's biography are that his family was Jewish and that he was a Shakespearean actor. Beyond the testimony of the plays themselves, this is the only solid justification for the remarks which follow. But even if this critic's tenuous notions about parallels and narrative sources at conscious or subconscious levels are in error, they may still open up new perspectives on the work at hand.

The narrative and thematic source which *The Homecoming* most immediately suggests is Christ's parable of "the prodigal son." Indeed, it would be difficult to explore the idea of "homecoming" without suggesting this narrative sequence in one way or another, so deeply imbedded is it in the Christian consciousness. In an age which seems to have few myths which can act as common denominators for human experience, the myth of "the prodigal" stands out as one of the few having a fairly universal coinage.

Nevertheless, there are elements in the play which suggest that the relationships are particular and not general. The prodigal son returned, it will be remembered, having "wasted his substance with riotous living" and "devoured his living with harlots": "And when he had spent all, there arose a mighty famine in that land; and he began to be in want." Teddy and Ruth have conflicting stories to tell about America. Teddy refers to the good life, the sun, their lovely house, and the "stimulating" environment. But, for Ruth, it is something else entirely. Her description suggests a land of famine, a land of plagues, such as those visited upon the Egyptians. The "cuddle and kiss" which Max insists upon at the Act One curtain suggests the compassion which the father in the parable showed towards his son (though Max's feelings here are clearly not compassionate), and Max's occupation as a butcher and his constant emphasis on blood suggests the killing of a fatted calf. There is no evidence that Teddy has wasted his substance in riotous living; nevertheless,

[4] Harold Pinter and Hallam Tennyson, Interview, B.B.C. General Overseas Service (August 7, 1960).

he has had to do with "harlots," has even married one, and for this sin he is in due time forgiven with rather alarming consequences.

The real significance of the "prodigal" theme, however, lies not in the comparison but in the contrast. Teddy's fate is opposed to that of the figure in the parable; we wonder, in fact, if he is not perhaps the fatted calf in this version of the celebration. At the conclusion of the play's "merry-making," Teddy is lost and not found, dead and not alive. In fact, Ruth seems to have forgotten his name in the last line she speaks to him: "Eddie. Don't become a stranger." The ostensible hero is transformed into a *pharmakos,* or scapegoat, a transformation with which we are familiar from Pinter's earlier plays.

There seems to be, however, a more complex Biblical parallel involved which relies on a less familiar narrative sequence. Ruth's name may suggest the Biblical Ruth, but few of us are conversant enough with the Old Testament story to make the proper connections. At most, we shall probably recall that she was a Gentile who returned to Israel with her mother-in-law, Naomi, saying: "Thy people shall be my people, and thy God my God." Even this, however, particularly the relevance of her statement to the action of the play, ought to alert us to the possible significance of the parallel.

In the Biblical narrative, Ruth is a Moabite and the widow of Mahlon, Naomi's son. Upon her return to Bethlehem with Naomi, she goes into the fields to work, where she meets Boaz, a kinsman of her late husband, who speaks kindly to her. According to Israelite law, the brother-in-law of a childless widow, or the next nearest of kin, was required to marry her in order to insure the perpetuation of the family strain. Ruth, at her mother-in-law's instigation, goes to the threshing floor where Boaz is working and, while he is asleep, lies down at his feet, asserting her claim to him by means of an old custom:

> And it came to pass at midnight, that the man was afraid, and turned himself: and, behold, a woman lay at his feet. And he said, Who art thou? And she answered, I am Ruth thine handmaid: spread therefore thy skirt over thine handmaid; for thou art a near kinsman.

He agrees to perform the "kinsman's part" for her, if another, who is yet more closely related, refuses. The nearer kinsman declines, saying: "I cannot redeem it for myself, lest I mar my own inheritance." Boaz and Ruth are married:

> And Boaz said unto the elders, and unto all the people, Ye are witnesses this day, that . . . Ruth the Moabitess, the wife of Mahlon, have I purchased to be my wife, to raise up the name of the dead upon his inheritance, that the name of the dead be not cut off from among his brethren, and from the gate of his place: ye are witnesses this day.

If the parable of the prodigal son helps us to understand Teddy's role in the dramatic fable, the history of Ruth provides clues to Ruth's actions and to the strange behavior which her appearance seems to induce in the other characters. Both Ruths are aliens; both seem to make a "claim" upon their kinsmen; and the midnight encounter with Boaz on the threshing floor parallels Ruth's strange midnight encounter with Lenny in *The Homecoming* which concludes with Lenny aware that "some kind of a proposal" has been made.

Besides illuminating the motives which are operating behind some of the play's more difficult moments, the comparison makes clear the ambivalence of Ruth's position. In terms of the family, she is, like the Biblical Ruth, a Gentile and a heathen, by definition unclean and contaminated. Since such religious distinctions have no place in the play, an objective correlative must be found to express her "Gentility." She becomes, therefore, a whore, a "smelly scrubber," a "pox-ridden slut," in order to be redeemed from that state and accepted as "kith and kin" of the chosen people. (Again, the ironic inversion: Ruth becomes a whore in order to truly belong.) At the conclusion of the play, the redemption has taken place. In fact, Ruth sits enthroned like a queen among her subjects, repository of the seed from which kings will emerge. In this guise, she has also saved the family from sterility and will perpetuate the strain. Max seems to be unpleasantly aware of this transformation; hence, his final agonized concern over whether she has understood what they expect from her, and his attempt to re-establish the functional bond which was the basis of the agreement. Which is Ruth? The subservient whore? Or the frozen mythic princess whom the characters have unwittingly created and to whom they have unwittingly ceded their male dominion?

Whether or not these Biblical parallels are operative, there is little question that the dramatic world which Pinter conjures up has unusual affinities with the Judaic tradition—just as Kafka's world has. The family unit, as something to be revered and feared, lies at the center of this world. It acts both as a secure haven and as a threat from within, asserting its claim upon its members, frequently with violence. Pinter's world is equally a world of commandments, laws, and rules which one breaks only at one's peril.

The comparison between *The Homecoming* and Shakespeare's *Troilus and Cressida* could be made simply on the basis of a resemblance in tone and attitude. Both plays are unequivocal in their unmasking of hypocrisy and false value. Shakespeare takes a heroic and romantic story and proceeds to write an intensely anti-heroic and anti-romantic play. The noble Achilles murders a defenseless Hector and ties the corpse to his horse's tail. The Greek leaders are portrayed as buffoons and perverts, and Helen as a vapid nonentity. Pinter's play is not ostensibly heroic, but it is decked in the full regalia of cherished values, memories, and traditions which are exposed to an equally dyspeptic scrutiny.

Beyond this, however, there are again points of comparison which seem more than accidental. Most striking is Cressida's welcome to the Greek camp as a hostage:

> *Agamemnon.* Most dearly welcome to the Greeks, sweet lady.
> *Nestor.* Our general doth salute you with a kiss.
> *Ulysses.* Yet is the kindness but particular; 'Twere better she were kissed in general.

In accordance with Ulysses' punning suggestion, she is passed from Greek to Greek, and each claims a kiss from her. (Ruth, as a hostage of Teddy's family, undergoes a similar initiation with equal willingness.) Later, Troilus and Ulysses spy on Cressida as she flirts with the Greek, Diomedes, with the omnipresent Thersites providing ironic commentary:

> *Troilus.* Cressid comes forth to him.
> *Diomedes.* How now, my charge?

Cressida. Now, my sweet guardian! Hark, a word with you. (*Whispers.*)

Troilus. Yea, so familiar?

Ulysses. She will sing any man at first sight.

Thersites. And any man may sing her, if he can take her cliff; she's noted.

Diomedes. Will you remember? . . .

Cressida. In faith, I cannot: what would you have me do?

Thersites. A juggling trick,—to be secretly open.

Similar scenes in which the sexual urge is exposed in a cruel and unromantic light are to be found in *The Homecoming:*

Joey. Christ, she's wide open. Dad, look at that. (*Pause.*) She's a tart.

* * *

Max. Where's the whore? Still in bed? She'll make us all animals.

Lenny. The girl's a tease.

* * *

Lenny. I've got a better idea. Why don't I take her up with me to Greek Street? (*Pause.*)

Max. You mean put her on the game? (*Pause.*) We'll put her on the game. That's a stroke of genius, that's a marvelous idea. You mean she can earn the money herself—on her back?

Teddy, like Troilus, is compelled to witness scenes which must curdle his blood, scenes in which the woman he calls wife is pawed, kissed, prostituted, and profaned. Ruth, like Cressida, is a Trojan among the Greeks (again the "alien" theme), and a Trojan who makes herself a Greek by using her sex as bait. At the play's conclusion, she is relegated, like Cressida, to Greek Street.

Out of a discussion between Lenny and Teddy on the subject of being and non-being, a matter which Teddy says "doesn't fall within my province," comes an opaque and disturbing statement by Ruth:

> Don't be too sure though. You've forgotten something. Look at me. I . . . move my leg. That's all it is. But I wear . . . underwear . . . which moves with me . . . it . . . captures your attention. Perhaps you misinterpret. The action is simple. It's a leg . . . moving. My lips move. Why don't you restrict your observations to that? Perhaps the fact that they move is more significant . . . than the words which come through them. You must bear that . . . possibility . . . in mind.

Is she referring to a language of the body, a sensual communication which words cannot approximate? Ulysses ascribes just such a language to Cressida in startingly similar terms:

> Fie, fie upon her!
> There's language in her eye, her cheek, her lip,
> Nay, her foot speaks, her wanton spirits look out
> At every joint and motive of her body.
> O these encounterers, so glib of tongue,
> That give a coasting welcome ere it comes,
> And wide unclasp the tables of their thoughts
> To every ticklish reader! set them down
> For sluttish spoils of opportunity,
> And daughters of the game.

It is worth noting in passing that "the game" in Pinter and Shakespeare has a similar reference, and that both Ruth and Cressida play by the same rules.

Earlier, I remarked upon the state of trance in which Ruth seems to drift through so much of the play, a kind of hypnosis presumably imposed upon her by the naked wills of the men among whom she moves. Early in the first scene of the play, Max remarks upon his "instinctive understanding of animals," particularly of fillies, and suggests that some hypnotic effect is involved. Cressida uses hypnosis as an excuse for her unavoidable wantonness:

> Troilus, farewell! one eye looks on thee,
> But with my heart the other eye doth see.
> Ah, poor our sex! this fault in us I find
> The error of our eye directs our mind:
> What error leads must err; O, then conclude
> Minds swayed by eyes are full of turpitude.

There would seem to be sufficient evidence that the two plays are preoccupied with similar images and concerns and that the atmosphere which they generate and the attitude which they project seem to have much in common. In addition, we can see that Cressida among the Greeks, Ruth among the Israelites, and the heroine of *The Homecoming* among her husband's family are all wanderers who, to borrow a phrase from Keats, stand "in tears amid the alien corn."

It would perhaps be better to discard the idea of narrative parallels in the play as having altogether the wrong implications. If the prodigal son, the Biblical Ruth, and Shakespeare's Greeks and Trojans are all validly related to Pinter's latest play, the notion of "parallels" becomes difficult to support. In the myth of the prodigal, there is no place for Ruth. In the story of Ruth, there is no place for Teddy. In *Troilus and Cressida* there is room for both, but this "parallel" excludes the Judaic frame of reference which seems so vital to the play.

What is perhaps most important is the recognition that Ruth is a "fractionized" image forced into completely contradictory roles: mother and whore, wife and sister, matriarch and handmaiden, guardian and hostage. At the height of his agony, while watching Cressida betray him, Troilus suddenly sees her as two Cressida's, one his and one Diomedes':

> This she? no, this is Diomed's Cressida: . . .
> If there be rules in unity itself,
> This was not she. O madness of discourse,
> That cause sets up with and against itself!

Erich Kahler in *The Tower and the Abyss* speaks of the "disintegration of the individual" as being characteristic of our age. The "unity and integrity of the human form," which is perhaps the primary value which we have been bequeathed by Greek and Jewish antiquity, has been broken down, subjected to a "dissolution of coherence and structure." [5] What Kahler refers to as "fractionized universe" and "fractionized consciousness" is evident not only in contemporary art but also in a host of Shakespearean characters, Hamlet, the two Richards, Cressida, among others who, submitted to "bi-fold authority" and conflicting claims upon them, divide "more wider than the sky and earth," although "the spacious breadth of this division/Admits no orifex for a point as subtle/As Ariachna's broken woof to enter." Pinter's characters frequently show the same divisions, and it is this fact, in addition to a similarly powerful verbal complexity and sense of structure, which gives his plays their texture and vitality.

[5] Erich Kahler, *The Tower and the Abyss* (New York: George Braziller, Inc., 1957), p. xiv.

IV

> "But you . . . Ruth . . . you're kin. You're Kith. You belong here."

In effect, what *The Homecoming* finally illustrates is the triumph of function over blood tie. As early as *The Birthday Party,* a struggle-to-the-death between the community (or family), and the collectivity (or organization) seemed to be a central issue in Pinter's work. The family bases its judgment of belonging on blood. The collectivity bases its judgment of belonging on function. In *The Caretaker,* Davies' attempt to take on a function as "caretaker" is defeated by his inability to deal with the blood tie between the two brothers. *The Homecoming* illustrates the process in reverse. The blood tie is set aside; the family has no "need" for a Ph.D.: what it does need is a woman and it simply takes what it needs. A prodigal attempts to reclaim his family and is turned away, but his wife is initiated into the tribe, becoming "kith" and "kin."

The idea represented by the phrase, "kith and kin," is of immense importance to the play. "Kin," of course, denotes blood relationship. Originally, however, "kith" denoted countryman rather than blood relative; it stems from the same root as "couth," and both refer to what is "known" by the beholder. It may not be wide of the mark to say that Teddy is kin but not kith (related but not known), and Ruth kith but not kin. At the end of the play, Teddy has been rejected from both circles, but Max warmly accepts Ruth as "kith" and "kin," separating the phrase into its two component parts to make a significant effect.

"Blood" also runs through the play as a persistent image. It serves a double function, since it is the strongest expression of the family tie and also a by-product of the butcher's trade. The curious scene in which Ruth offers Lenny a drink from her water-glass may be a distortion of the Jewish marriage rite; it can also be viewed as a reference to the traditional proverb: "Blood is thicker than water."

Related to the play's immersion in the world of the family is its ironic contemplation of values. Max and Lenny talk about values constantly. Both—but particularly Lenny—speak on this subject with such confidence that we tend to be taken in. The very mention of "values" tends to intimidate us. Pinter, however, places these references in juxtaposition with actions by the same characters which refute any notion of moral ultimatums. Max refers to Ruth as a woman of "quality" and "feeling" as she is in the process of rolling off the couch with Joey. Max's description of his dead wife as a "slutbitch," is succeeded by the statement that "she taught them [i.e., Teddy, Lenny, Joey] all the morality they know."

In the second act, Lenny launches into the play's fullest statement of family values, in response to Teddy's admission that he has stolen Lenny's cheese roll. Since the family is already well advanced in the process of stealing Teddy's wife, concern over a cheese roll at this moment seems somewhat profane. There is an ironic displacement involved here; by all rights, this should be Teddy's speech in response to the gross indignities to which he has been submitted:

> Barefaced audacity. (*Pause.*) What led you to be so . . . vindictive against your own brother? I'm bowled over.
>
> * * *
>
> Well, if that's the kind of thing they teach you over there, you're welcome to it, Ted. But I think in that case you'd better cut your visits to this country down to a bare minimum. After all, we're talking about kith and kin, aren't we? I mean that's what we're talking about.
>
> * * *
>
> Because we know something about the values which have been handed down to us. . . . Our little community, our little group, our team, you might say, our unit, made up of, I'll admit it, various and not entirely similar component parts, but which, put together, do nevertheless make up a whole. An organization, which, though we're not exactly a sentimental family, we do recognize as such. And you're an integral part of it, Ted. . . . And so when you at length return to us, we do expect a bit of grace, a bit of liberality of spirit, to reassure us. We do expect that. But do we get it? Have we got it? Is that what you've given us?

There is no question that Lenny is upset about his cheese roll; the act of theft has disordered his world; chaos has been invited to institute its reign. Again, an echo from *Troilus and Cressida* is helpful, Ulysses' much quoted speech on "degree," a speech which is also a defense of traditional values and which comes from just as unlikely a source:

> The heavens themselves, the planets and this centre,
> Observe degree, priority and place,
> Insisture, course, proportion, season, form,
> Office and custom, in all line of order: . . . .
> Take but degree away, untrue that string,
> And, hark, what discord follows! each thing melts
> In mere oppugnancy: . . . .
> Force should be right; or rather, right and wrong,
> Between whose endless jar justice resides,
> Should lose their names, and so should justice too.
> Then every thing include itself in power.
> Power into will, will into appetite;
> And appetite, an universal wolf . . .
> Must make perforce an universal prey,
> And last eat up himself.

The last three lines seem a fitting précis for *The Homecoming*.

The concept of family which Max and Lenny have is clearly a collage of empty clichés. Responsibility, democracy, morality, quality, standards, feeling, values, liberality of spirit, and generosity of mind: words, words, words. But beneath the verbal gloss, as beneath a politician's panaceas, what we see in the attitudes and responses of the characters and in their relationships to each other is a reality which is prehistoric and primitive, a world where appetite reigns. Max's stick defends him against the murderous impulses of his sons; a woman is dragged into the cave and the inhabitants argue over their share in her as if she were a piece of meat; images of blood and butchery predominate; any respect for the value of human life is belied. Beneath the stated values of the play, there is a total absence of values, a void which is filled by the human family's animal struggle to survive and perpetuate itself. That such an environment should spawn a Doctor of Philosophy is one of the more brutal ironies of a play which exposes the powerlessness of rationality. *The Homecoming* makes us aware that Pinter is again showing us nothing more surprising or mystifying than man's primitive nature reasserting itself, naked and demanding, from beneath the layers of intellectual and ethical sophistication with which it has been so carefully covered.

The English Stage

by Robert Brustein

An American visitor to London is dazzled by theatrical illuminations that shine even more brightly by contrast with our own darkling stage. America now has an ever-growing number of permanent companies, and some of them can boast of considerable achievements. But it will be a long time, I fear, before we can begin to match the adventurousness of the Royal Shakespeare Company at the Aldwych, the fine, fearless integrity of the English Stage Society at the Royal Court, or the expertise of the National Theatre at the Old Vic. There is something in the American character that has thus far proved resistant to collective artistic enterprise—something at the same time invigorating (an anarchic independence of will) and degenerate (a selfish opportunism)—with the result that our serious theatre has been continually engaged in an exhausting struggle with the frailties that are always threatening to destroy it, whether reflected in the actor's glory-lust, the producer's venality, the designer's self-indulgence, the director's careerism, or the spectator's fatigue and apathy.

That these frailties are also operative in the English theatre, I have the word of some English theatre critics, but once away from the West End, they are not immediately visible to a visitor's naked eye—the quality, and even the quantity, of British permanent companies testify to a flourishing theatrical health. The new English drama, however, seems to me somewhat less robust at the moment. As a movement, it appears to be temporarily stalled, and it has yet to realise the promise of its auspicious beginnings. Osborne, Pinter, Wesker, Jellicoe, Arden, Delaney, Owen and the rest of the 'new realists' are continuing to turn out a substantial number of plays, some of which excite a good deal of interest; and there is no doubt that these plays are still much fresher and more energetic than the work of those who previously dominated the English stage—Coward, Rattigan and Fry, for example. Furthermore, the new drama has engendered a breed of actors who, for sheer power, breadth and truthfulness, are now unmatched in the English-speaking world, not to mention a company of designers who have brought a powerful abstract simplicity to costume and stage settings. Still, despite such achievements, few of these writers have proceeded very far beyond their initial phase of development, and none, to my mind, has turned into an artist of the first rank.

To substantiate this controversial charge, and to find some reasons for it, one must turn to historical parallels, and there is an obvious analogy to be made between the English drama of the past decade and the American drama of the Thirties. In each case, new playwrights emerged in significant numbers out of social-political ferment; and in each case, they found their identity less as inspired individuals than as members of a movement with specific social goals. The new English drama is, admittedly, superior to the American social drama of the Thirties (which left nothing of lasting value, not even the work of Odets), but it has a similar coloration, being more impressive as a cultural phenomenon than as a unique artistic force. And it is equally restricted by the very conditions that originally gave it life. The revolution that recently swept across the English stage succeeded in clearing away the debris of artificial drawing-room comedies, sterile well-made plays and vacant pseudo-Elizabethan poetic dramas, but like the social revolution in Depression America it created an ideological atmosphere in which many began to regard the drama as a weapon of class warfare. Fewer English than American playwrights have accepted these ideological roles with equanimity—some, notably Harold Pinter, have even vigorously repudiated them—but only one or two have managed to extricate themselves entirely from class interests and stand alone as free and independent artists.

The result is apparent in the new plays, many of which reek

with sentimentality about the working class, excessive literalism, over-insistence on the grime and squalor of Midlands industrial cities, stale didacticism, and a kind of laziness about working out a theme in action. The result is also apparent in the writings of the critics, theorists and polemicists who, like the Marxist critics of the Thirties, have been exhorting the new drama since its beginnings. This latter company has been gathered together in a recent volume called *The Encore Reader*[1]—an anthology of articles from the influential little magazine of the theatre, *Encore*. Subtitled 'A Chronicle of the New Drama,' this volume embodies both the virtues and the failings of the movement it examines: it is bursting with energy, vigour, and excitement, and it is seriously lacking in balanced judgments or penetrating ideas.

One is struck, first and foremost, by a feeling of embattlement: each new article is a gauntlet, each new play a war game. The complicated issues of art tend to dissolve into simple oppositions: Socialism versus Toryism, the new versus the old, experiment versus tradition, the proletariat versus the upper classes, youth versus age —and everyone connected with the theatre is neatly catalogued. If an old lady expresses what to some would be an understandable indifference to a play of Arnold Wesker, then this, the writer speculates, is because Wesker 'came too close to life, dealt with actual problems, felt strongly about them, and wanted to impel his audience to do something about them.' Another writer, discussing Osborne's debacle, *The World of Paul Slickey,* assumes without hesitation that its sour reception was motivated by hostility to the New Left, even though he eventually forces himself to concede that the play is dismal.

Not all of the articles are so narrow, for the policy of the magazine is much less doctrinaire than some of its contributors. At the same time that Lindsay Anderson is demanding ideological rigidity, arguing that *Encore* should print not 'every point of view,' but only 'the right one,' John Whiting is also questioning the intellectual and artistic value of socialist plays. And while some writers are advising modern dramatists to eliminate despair from their plays, accentuate the positive, and point the way towards utopian

[1] *The Encore Reader,* ed. Charles Marowitz, Tom Milne, and Owen Hale (London: Methuen & Co., Ltd., 1965).

social goals (shades of Soviet realism!), others are extolling the virtues of such non-political, non-affirming writers as Beckett, Genet, Ionesco, Artaud, and even such a disaffected comic anarchist as Lenny Bruce. When a gifted playwright or performer is being defended against the uncomprehending hostility of snobs and philistines, or when artistic achievements are being examined in depth, then *The Encore Reader* performs a valuable critical function. But just as frequently the tenor of the anthology is cranky and contentious, while its tone tends to alternate between the shrill and the hoarse. Hospitality is extended to naifs like Eli Wallach, discoursing inarticulately on the eloquence of the Method, and to egos from the film world like Joseph Losey, discussing Brecht's 'influence on me' (and vice versa). Brecht himself is admired for what seem to me all the wrong reasons, and is, therefore, continually lumped together with a lesser writer like Arthur Miller, presumably because both deal in social-political problems. Familiar opinions on questions of race, sex and society are paraded as advanced in a self-righteous manner recalling Roebuck Ramsden's liberalism; and finally, too much of the book is given over to garbled logic, ringing manifestoes, utilitarian demands, questionable motive-hunting, fuzzy theories and downright bad prose.

I make these complaints as a friend of the house, and would in fact be less disturbed about these writers if I weren't so profoundly sympathetic with most of their aims. But their aims have now been largely achieved and, as so often happens with successful revolutionaries, their excesses now seem to be institutionalised, ossifying into postures that should be more supple and flexible. Chief among these is a certain indifference to poetry, imagination, form and dialectic in the drama, and a partiality to plays that propagandise for change (this last demand, explicit in many articles in the anthology, is seconded by Kenneth Tynan in a long interview). What *The Encore Reader* finally lacks is a sense of critical disinterestedness. It does not advance dramatic art to defend bad plays because they support your prejudices, or to tolerate nitwittery for the sake of a Cause, or to reprimand playwrights for failing to deal with their economic and political environment. Overly permissive in one sense, the *Encore* critics have been overly restrictive in another, so that one comes away grateful for what they have accomplished in the way of supporting experimental playwrights, but dubious about their ultimate value to the movement of English drama as a whole.

This uncertainty increases when one looks at the movement itself. For while the new English playwrights have certainly proved less simplistic politically than most of their supporters (at least in their work), they nevertheless strike similar doctrinal postures. These, to be sure, are relatively implicit, being suggested less through direct appeals than through certain significant choices (thematic concerns, types of characters, theatrical style); but they are clearly responsible, in my opinion, for certain impediments to genuine advance. Despite an occasional leavening of epic technique from Brecht, for example, the dominant style of recent English drama has been social realism; and while this style may seem unusual to audiences conditioned by frothy commodities from Shaftesbury Avenue, it has long been exhausted as a medium for fresh dramatic insight and long been abandoned by the more adventurous dramatists of Europe. The English commitment to an old-fashioned style is accompanied by an infatuation with what one *Encore* writer calls 'the gritty realities of working-class life.' This also has its unfortunate side since, at the same time that it opens up an area of experience long ignored or patronised by English playwrights, it inspires another form of class consciousness—a species of inverted snobbery only slightly less offensive than the old.

Two English dramatists are relatively free of such limitations—Harold Pinter, who (perhaps in reaction against the sermonising of his colleagues) excludes statement from his work altogether, and John Arden, who has managed to preserve a certain unpredictability. Both offer hope for future growth and development (though Pinter has recently been repeating himself). One cannot be entirely sanguine, however, about the other members of the movement. Take the case of Arnold Wesker, a writer who seems to exaggerate all its worst faults. Let us pass over his irrepressible impulse to indoctrinate the working classes with Higher Forms of Art, though this may some day constitute one of the most embarrassing episodes in recent English cultural history. His plays are a good deal more complicated about such missions than his behaviour warrants, and when he deals—in the *Chicken Soup* trilogy and in *Chips With Everything*—with the intellectual's poignant failure to merge with the masses, he uncorks a theme which is both convincing and deeply felt. His writing, on the other hand, though full of sincerity, is almost completely wanting in art, being crude, zealous, garrulous and naive; his sense of style has not developed much beyond the grey, exacting realism of Galsworthy; and his relentless missionary temperament and perennial innocence frequently turn his characters into caricatures from agit-prop.

Or take the case of John Osborne, who originated the new movement and who remains its most showy figure. Osborne is unquestionably a born dramatist, and his vocabulary of invective is simply stunning, but I think he has yet to write a work that will endure. Too much of his writing remains unformulated, and too much remains unfinished; his plays have the quality of electrical particles without a nucleus to hold them in orbit. Osborne's dramatic discipline since *Epitaph for George Dillon* has grown increasingly loose, and more and more he has begun to indulge a weakness for dramatic ventriloquism: *Inadmissible Evidence,* for example, after a brilliant first act, collapses completely into structural chaos, as the author introduces rhetorical essays on subjects only remotely related to his theme. The typical Osborne scene consists of one person orating and another listening—the monologues are inspired but they do not admit of true argument. And he is capable, I think, of writing only one character fully: the cruel, blistering protagonist who evokes the spectator's pity when he reveals himself to be collapsing under the burden of his own unpleasantness. This suggests that under the hard veneer of Osborne's style there lurks considerable sentimentality, and makes it understandable why he has been successful on Broadway when the more radical dramatists from France cannot make it through the back door. Until Osborne can put his wonderful eloquence at the service of consistently worked-out themes, he will remain a playwright of the second rank.

I realise that I have been extremely harsh towards writers who are now a source of considerable national pride. But the whole development of recent English drama inspires an American with a sense of *déjà vu.* What began for us in a similar way—as a radical theatre movement tied to a radical politics—eventually became the standard form of our commercial stage, and American drama ever since has been trying to break loose from this debilitating inheritance. I suspect that because English audiences have been traditionally Tory, English playwrights have assumed a correspondence between a left-wing politics and an advanced drama; but Americans can testify, to their regret, that no such correspondence exists—quite the contrary, our own politically liberal drama has been responsible for glib affirmations, simple-minded melodramas and self-congratulatory conventions.

What most of the great modern dramatists have understood (and even Brecht and Shaw, I believe, understood it secretly) is that whatever his personal affiliations, the writer must remain independent in his art—that even political plays must be free from partisanship—for when the drama becomes an instrument of utility or the captive of a creed, it is condemned and sacrificed. Theatrical conditions are marvellous in England at present, the nation's recent dramatic achievement is substantial, and when it comes to raw playwriting talent, it can compete with any country in the world. But English drama is now in some danger of dissipating its possibilities in the service of causes unconnected with the free imagination. On most subjects, Americans can tell the English very little, but in this case we have been there before you. It would be a pity if you could not build on our mistakes.

Chronology of Important Dates

1929	Birth of John Osborne in London.
1930	Birth of Harold Pinter in Hackney, London.
	Birth of John Arden in Barnsley, Yorkshire.
1932	Birth of Arnold Wesker in Stepney, London.
1955	First performance of Samuel Beckett's *Waiting for Godot* at the Arts Theatre, and, later, Criterion Theatre, London.
1956	First performance of *Look Back in Anger* at the Royal Court Theatre, London, and the Lyric Theatre, Hammersmith.
1957	First performance of *The Entertainer* at the Royal Court Theatre, London.
1958	First performance of *The Birthday Party* at the Lyric Theatre, Hammersmith.
1959	First performance of *The Kitchen* at the Royal Court Theatre, London.
	First performance of *Serjeant Musgrave's Dance* at the Royal Court Theatre, London.
1960	First performance of *The Caretaker* at the Arts and Duchess Theatres, London.
	First performance at the Royal Court Theatre, London, of the trilogy, *Chicken Soup with Barley, Roots,* and *I'm Talking About Jerusalem* (by the Belgrade Theatre Company of Coventry).
	First performance of *The Happy Haven* at the Royal Court Theatre, London (after production at the Drama Department of the University of Bristol).
1961	First performance of *Luther* at the Royal Court and Phoenix Theatres, London.
1962	First performance of *Chips with Everything* at the Royal Court and Vaudeville Theatres, London.
1963	First performance of *The Workhouse Donkey* at the Chichester Festival Theatre.

1964 First performance of *Inadmissible Evidence* at the Royal Court Theatre, London (transferring to Wyndham's Theatre in 1965).

1965 First performance of *The Homecoming* at the Aldwych Theatre, London (by the Royal Shakespeare Company).

First performance of *Armstrong's Last Goodnight* at the Old Vic Theatre, London (by the National Theatre, after production at the Chichester Festival).

1966 First performance of *Their Very Own and Golden City* at the Royal Court Theatre, London.

Notes on the Editor and Contributors

JOHN RUSSELL BROWN, the editor of this volume, is Head of the Department of Drama and Theatre Arts at the University of Birmingham. He has directed professional and student productions of many contemporary plays, including several productions of plays by Beckett and Pinter. He is author of *Shakespeare's Plays in Performance.*

ROBERT BRUSTEIN is Dean of the Yale Drama School. Previously he was drama critic for *The New Republic* and taught at Columbia University, New York. His essays have appeared in *Harpers, Partisan Review, The Hudson Review,* and other journals, and he is author of *The Theatre of Revolt.* His drama criticism has been collected in *Seasons of Discontent.*

A. E. DYSON teaches English Literature at the University of East Anglia, Norwich. With C. B. Cox, he founded and now edits *The Critical Quarterly,* and together these scholars are preparing a three-volume history, *The Twentieth-Century Mind.* Mr. Dyson is author of *The Crazy Fabric: Essays in Irony.*

MARTIN ESSLIN is in charge of the Radio Drama Department of the British Broadcasting Corporation; he is also script reader for the Royal Shakespeare Company. He is the author of *Brecht: A Choice of Evils* and *The Theatre of the Absurd,* and the editor of *Beckett: A Collection of Critical Essays.*

RICHARD GILMAN is a contributing editor for *The New Republic*; previously he was drama critic for *The Commonweal* and has contributed to *Theatre Arts, Tulane Drama Review* and *The Saturday Review.*

ALBERT HUNT teaches at the Regional College of Art, Bradford. He has written frequently in *Encore* and other journals, and was an assistant to Peter Brook for directing the Royal Shakespeare Company's documentary program, *US.*

LAURENCE KITCHIN teaches in the Department of Drama at the University of Bristol; previously he trained and worked as an actor before becoming drama critic for the London *Times*. He is author of *Mid-Century Theatre* and *Drama in the Sixties*.

CHARLES MAROWITZ was an editor of *Encore* and has often written on theatrical subjects there and in *Tulane Drama Review* and *Plays and Players*. He has directed many plays in London and elsewhere; these include *The Theatre of Cruelty* experimental program for the Royal Shakespeare Company and Joe Orton's *Loot* at the Criterion.

TOM MILNE is Associate Editor of the international film magazine *Sight and Sound*; previously he was Editor and frequent contributor to *Encore*.

HUGH NELSON has taught in the Drama Department of San Jose State College of the University of California and previously studied at the Carnegie Institute of Technology, Pittsburgh. He has directed numerous university productions and has published poetry in the United States and Great Britain. He is now in charge of drama at McGill University, Montreal.

JOHN RUSSELL TAYLOR is film critic of the London *Times*. He is a drama critic for *Plays and Players* and a contributor to *London Magazine, Sight and Sound,* and other journals. He has published a study of Art Nouveau book illustration and *The Penguin Dictionary of the Theatre*.

RAYMOND WILLIAMS, Fellow of Jesus College Cambridge and University Lecturer in English Literature, is author of *Culture and Society 1780-1950, Drama from Isben to Eliot, The Long Revolution, Modern Tragedy,* and *Border Country: a Novel,* etc.

Selected Bibliography

Peter Davison, "Contemporary Drama and Popular Dramatic Forms," *Aspects of Drama and the Theatre* (Sydney: Sydney University Press, 1965), pp. 143-97. Parallels between new drama and music hall, pantomime, and popular radio and television entertainment are used to raise problems of interpretation and performance.

The Encore Reader, ed. Charles Marowitz, Tom Milne and Owen Hale (London: Methuen & Co., Ltd., 1965). Reprints articles from the British theatrical periodical which was the platform for new ideas during the '50s and early '60s.

Martin Esslin, *The Theatre of the Absurd* (London: Eyre & Spottiswoode, 1961; New York: Doubleday and Company, 1961). A philosophical and critical study of European theatre; sections on Beckett, Pinter, and Simpson are especially important for British theatre.

Experimental Drama, ed. W. A. Armstrong (London: G. Bell and Sons, 1963). The best single volume for following up the interests of this collection: it includes studies of regional playwrights and of Osborne, Bolt, and Whiting; there is an important chapter by the editor on theatre management.

Richard Findlater, *The Unholy Trade* (London: Victor Gollancz, 1952). A brilliant, comprehensive, and influential account of English theatre practice at the beginning of the 1950s; it is still an indispensable background book.

Bamber Gascoigne, *Twentieth Century Drama* (London: Hutchinson University Library, 1962). A clear account of drama since 1900, with its main focus on the British theatre; a good introduction despite short measure on the most recent drama.

Laurence Kitchin, *Drama in the Sixties: Form and Interpretation* (London: Faber and Faber, Ltd., 1966). An account of English theatre in the early '60s, including a number of reviews of performances of Shakespeare, etc.

Laurence Kitchin, *Mid-Century Theatre* (London: Faber and Faber, Ltd., 1960). Essays on actors, dramatists, and directors, followed by a series of interviews with theatrical figures first published in *The Times* of London.

Frederick Lumley, *New Trends in 20th Century Drama: A Survey since Isben and Shaw* (London: Barry and Rockliffe, second edition, 1967). The new edition of this introductory work adds a short but wide-ranging account of new British plays.

Stratford-upon-Avon Studies, 4: Contemporary Theatre, ed. John Russell Brown and Bernard Harris (London: Edward Arnold, 1962; New York: St. Martin's Press, 1962). Nine critics study aspects of the British Theatre since Bernard Shaw; the various chapters have been chosen to represent a wide range of critical method as well as diverse responsible judgments.

John Russell Taylor, *Anger and After: A Guide to the New British Drama* (London: Methuen & Co., Ltd., 1962). Also published as *The Angry Theatre* (New York: Hill and Wang, Inc., 1962). The most comprehensive account of the careers of new dramatists, including the plot outlines of many plays and a general description of theatrical conditions in Britain from the early '50s to 1961.

John Whiting, *John Whiting on Theatre* (London: Alan Ross, 1966). Collection of theatre reviews by the dramatist which originally appeared in *London Magazine.*

TWENTIETH CENTURY VIEWS

British Authors

S-TC-2 T. S. Eliot, edited by Hugh Kenner
S-TC-9 Fielding, edited by Ronald Paulson
S-TC-19 John Donne, edited by Helen Gardner
S-TC-22 Ben Jonson, edited by Jonas A. Barish
S-TC-23 Yeats, edited by John Unterecker
S-TC-24 D. H. Lawrence, edited by Mark Spilka
S-TC-25 Hardy, edited by Albert Guerard
S-TC-26 Jane Austen, edited by Ian Watt
S-TC-31 Byron, edited by Paul West
S-TC-32 Dryden, edited by Bernard N. Schilling
S-TC-35 Swift, edited by Ernest Tuveson
S-TC-40 Shakespeare: The Tragedies, edited by Alfred Harbage
S-TC-43 Keats, edited by Walter Jackson Bate
S-TC-44 Marlowe, edited by Clifford Leech
S-TC-45 Shakespeare: The Histories, edited by Eugene M. Waith
S-TC-47 Shakespeare: The Comedies, edited by Kenneth Muir
S-TC-48 Samuel Johnson, edited by Donald J. Greene
S-TC-49 Shelley, edited by George M. Ridenour
S-TC-50 G. B. Shaw, edited by R. J. Kaufmann
S-TC-53 Conrad, edited by Marvin Mudrich
S-TC-56 Dylan Thomas, edited by Charles B. Cox
S-TC-57 Hopkins, edited by Geoffrey H. Hartman
S-TC-58 Blake, edited by Northrop Frye
S-TC-59 Forster, edited by Malcom Bradbury
S-TC-60 Milton, edited by Louis L. Martz
S-TC-64 Restoration Dramatists, edited by Earl Miner
S-TC-70 Coleridge, edited by Kathleen Coburn
S-TC-72 Dickens, edited by Martin Price
S-TC-74 Modern British Dramatists, edited by John Russell Brown
S-TC-75 Thackeray, edited by Alexander Welsh
S-TC-77 Laurence Sterne, edited by John Traugott

TWENTIETH CENTURY VIEWS

American Authors

S-TC-3 ROBERT FROST, edited by James M. Cox
S-TC-5 WHITMAN, edited by Roy Harvey Pearce
S-TC-6 SINCLAIR LEWIS, edited by Mark Schorer
S-TC-8 HEMINGWAY, edited by Robert P. Weeks
S-TC-10 THOREAU, edited by Sherman Paul
S-TC-12 EMERSON, edited by Milton R. Konvitz
and Stephen E. Whicher
S-TC-13 MELVILLE, edited by Richard Chase
S-TC-20 EDITH WHARTON, edited by Irving Howe
S-TC-27 F. SCOTT FITZGERALD, edited by Arthur Mizener
S-TC-28 EMILY DICKENSON, edited by Richard B. Sewall
S-TC-29 EZRA POUND, edited by Walter Sutton
S-TC-30 MARK TWAIN, edited by Henry Nash Smith
S-TC-33 WALLACE STEVENS, edited by Marie Borroff
S-TC-34 HENRY JAMES, edited by Leon Edel
S-TC-38 AUDEN, edited by Monroe K. Spears
S-TC-39 O'NEILL, edited by John Gassner
S-TC-55 HAWTHORNE, edited by A. N. Kaul
S-TC-61 W. C. WILLIAMS, edited by J. Hillis Miller
S-TC-63 POE, edited by Robert Regan
S-TC-65 FAULKNER, edited by Robert Penn Warren
S-TC-66 STEPHEN CRANE, edited by Maurice Bassan
S-TC-69 MODERN AMERICAN DRAMATISTS, edited by Alvin B. Kernan